THE BOOK OF
MERMAID
magic

About the Author

©Daniel_sahnn/Daaniel Murillo-Vasquez

Leeza Robertson is an international best-selling author with Llewellyn Worldwide. She is a girl from the Aussie bush living her best life in Las Vegas, Nevada, with her wife. When she is not writing books or creating decks, she is helping other writers bring their dream of publishing into reality. Connect with Leeza on Instagram, Twitter, and Facebook.

To Write to the Author

If you wish to contact the author or would like more information about this book, please write to the author in care of Llewellyn Worldwide Ltd. and we will forward your request. Both the author and publisher appreciate hearing from you and learning of your enjoyment of this book and how it has helped you. Llewellyn Worldwide Ltd. cannot guarantee that every letter written to the author can be answered, but all will be forwarded. Please write to:

Leeza Robertson
℅ Llewellyn Worldwide
2143 Wooddale Drive
Woodbury, MN 55125-2989

Please enclose a self-addressed stamped envelope for reply, or $1.00 to cover costs. If outside the U.S.A., enclose an international postal reply coupon.

Many of Llewellyn's authors have websites with additional information and resources. For more information, please visit our website at http://www.llewellyn.com.

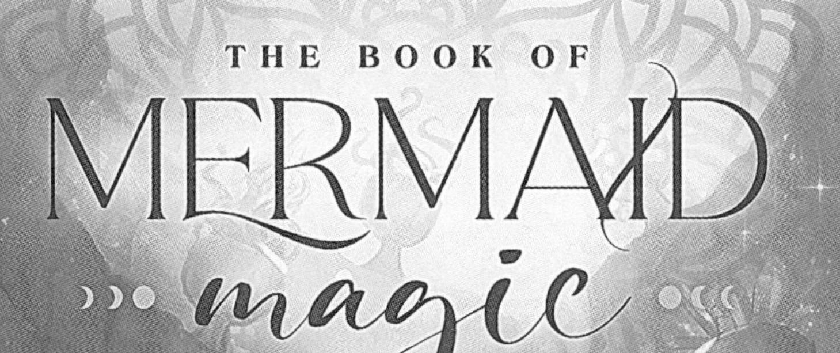

THE BOOK OF MERMAID *magic*

HEALING, SPELLWORK & CONNECTION WITH MERFOLK

LEEZA ROBERTSON

LLEWELLYN PUBLICATIONS | WOODBURY, MINNESOTA

First Edition
First Printing, 2023

Book design by Samantha Peterson
Cover art by Julie Dillon
Cover design by Cassie Willett
Interior art:
Chakra figure on page 8 by Mary Ann Zapalac
Tarot card art by Julie Dillon
Remaining art by Llewellyn Art Department

Library of Congress Cataloging-in-Publication Data
Names: Robertson, Leeza, author.
Title: The book of mermaid magic : healing, spellwork & connection with merfolk / Leeza Robertson.
Description: First edition. | Woodbury, Minnesota : Llewellyn Publications, 2022. | Summary: "With teachings as deep as the ocean, this book shows you how to find your own source of power and bring more abundance and happiness into your life" —Provided by publisher.
Identifiers: LCCN 2022038305 (print) | LCCN 2022038306 (ebook) | ISBN 9780738768519 (paperback) | ISBN 9780738768564 (ebook)
Subjects: LCSH: Magic. | Mermaids—Miscellanea. | Mermen—Miscellanea.
Classification: LCC BF1623.G63 R635 2022 (print) | LCC BF1623.G63 (ebook) | DDC 133.4/3—dc23/eng/20220909
LC record available at https://lccn.loc.gov/2022038305
LC ebook record available at https://lccn.loc.gov/2022038306

Llewellyn Publications
A Division of Llewellyn Worldwide Ltd.
2143 Wooddale Drive
Woodbury, MN 55125-2989
www.llewellyn.com

Printed in the United States of America

Other Books by Leeza Robertson

Animal Totem Tarot
Cirque du Tarot
The Divine Practice of Angel Numbers
Mermaid Tarot
Pathworking the Tarot
Soul Cats Tarot
Tarot Court Cards for Beginners
Tarot Healer
Tarot Priestess
Tarot Reversals for Beginners

Forthcoming Books by Leeza Robertson

A Year of Angel Guidance

This book is dedicated to all who hear the call of the water goddess. The landlocked mermaids who dream of the ocean and spend their lives in search of depth, meaning, and connection.

CONTENTS

Disclaimer

In the following pages you will find recommendations for the use of certain essential oils and ritual items. If you are allergic to any of these items, please refrain from use. Each body reacts differently to herbs, essential oils, and other items, so results may vary person to person.

Essential oils are potent; use care when handling them. Always dilute essential oils before placing them on your skin, and make sure to do a patch test on your skin before use. Perform your own research before using an essential oil.

INTRODUCTION

The call burst forth from the darkness below, pushed further by the rolling waves of the sea, mixing with the spray and seafoam. The notes echoed on the breeze, releasing the song into the world of the humans. To you, dear reader. Your mermaid ears were able to pluck the frequency out of the air. You heard the call. It called you to this book, to seek the guidance and wisdom your mermaid heart seeks, to get answers to questions that have been living in your soul. This call brought with it a need for connection, a connection to the part of you that yearns for the water yet lives upon the land. Inside of you is a mermaid heart just wanting to explore itself. Your mermaid heart, that piece of you that yearns for the water, needs to know who it is and how to express itself in the world of the two-legged. You see, many of us share this energy, this calling. This mermaid heart beats within you as a frequency, a vibration that is looking for a match—a mermaid match, if you will. That is what drew you to this book. I know this because I share the same heart.

Welcome, mermaid sibling. The mermaids and I honor your presence and greet you with open arms. The mermaids and I are so happy that you are here and ready to start a new journey with us. Just know that there are no myths, legends, and fantasies about mermaids in this book; this book is not another retelling of stories of old. Oh no. This book takes you inside the Mermaid Pantheon to introduce you to its members and to show you how to connect and work with each archetype to make your landlocked world a living prayer—one worthy of the water goddess herself. This is a devotional book, one that opens up the world of the merfolk for healing, spellwork, and deeper connection. You may even find your mermaid self inside the pages of this book: the mermaid self that has been flowing through you since you were born; the version of you that has a mermaid frequency tuned to the water, tuned to the goddess. For some, this may be your initiation into the realm of the merfolk. For others, this book will feel like coming home. Or maybe you are like me and have been very resistant to acknowledge this piece of yourself. I wasn't always this comfortable talking about mermaids. In fact, I thought it was all a bit much. I ignored the calls. I did my best to block out my yearning to be by the sea. I even denied my mermaid ways. Yet, despite all my doubts and denials, the mermaids still called, and my mermaid heart always heard them.

I remember the day I finally gave in to the call of the mermaids. I can still feel the rush of acceptance and excitement that washed over me like a crashing wave. It felt like finding home, even though it wasn't a physical place. My personal journey with the mermaids has been a long one, and in many ways I am still a little resistant. But I am more open to what they have to teach. They have taught me more about myself than I would have thought possible, and they've connected me to healing spaces that I would never have found on my own. To be honest, the mermaids have helped me level up and navigate my success. They've shown me when to use my energy, when to rest, when to ride the waves, and when to hide under the storming sea. Now, the mermaids and I offer this knowledge and wisdom to you, dear reader.

No matter where you are on your life journey, there is something in this book that can assist with your next steps. One of the mermaid archetypes might even hold the answer to a question your heart has been seeking. The archetypes in this book were designed by me—I feel that is important to point out. These archetypes are not something you will find in any other book; it is a system I created to help me work with the mermaids and their energy, messages, and lessons. You see, the more I started to let the mermaids into my meditation and eventually my life, I noticed they showed up in very specific forms. They tended to show up in one of the eight archetypes in this book. The more I noticed which archetype was showing up in my life, the easier it was to use the information I was receiving or to learn the lesson that would appear in my daily life. My hope is that this system will also work for you.

This book has more everyday, general tips and strategies as well, from how to bring calming energy into your day, to staying in the flow and motivated, to moving from feelings of overwhelm to feeling grounded and centered. Each chapter will explore a different theme, healing, and devotional practice as prescribed by the mermaid archetype that governs it, which in turn creates the Mermaid Pantheon.

Now, just a word before we go any further. Not all of those inside this pantheon will outwardly look like mermaids, but they are all part of the larger merfolk population, as they all fall under the label of water deity. In this book, I define the word *deity* as a supernatural being that has the magical skill to change, manipulate, or alter the world around them.

The archetypes I have created have been organized into a pantheon, which is a group of deities or important people in a society. Your Mermaid Pantheon includes, but is not limited to, the eight archetypes I have written about in this book. I arranged the archetypes based on hierarchy. The archetypes, in order from top to bottom, are:

1. The water goddess
2. The ocean priestess
3. The sea witch
4. The siren
5. The common mermaid
6. The shapeshifter
7. The nymph
8. The sprite

Each of these Mermaid Pantheon members has their own chapter. They tell their own story and have their own healing energy.

Even though this book may feel incredibly feminine by nature, I have not written it that way. For me, everything in this book is nonbinary. It is not limited to or contained by conventional masculine or feminine energy unless specified. The merfolk do not organize themselves into dual aspects of gender. Instead, they believe in personalized self-expression; they have a come-as-you-are type of philosophy when it comes to self-identification. This is how I invite you, dear reader, to work with the content and teachings in this book. Use it to expand your idea of who you are and how you wish to show up in the world. The merfolk want you to learn to open yourself up to love and your intuition, to create a life that is a living prayer, and to deepen your connection to yourself and your community. This is an embodied process, one that you get to decide on your own terms.

Swimming through the Chapters

It is time to dive deeper into what you will find inside this book. The way the content has been put together is very specific; it is arranged in a way that will maximize your experience with each of the mermaid archetypes. In each chapter, you will see there are four exercises for you to work through. Each one is designed to bring you a different experience with the deity you are immersing yourself with. I did not create these exercises randomly; these are the very exercises I personally use when connecting with the merfolk. These are the ways the merfolk have taught me the most, and that is the reason I have included them in this book. The exercises are:

Devotion: For the purposes of this book, we are using devotion work as a way to strengthen your connection with the deity. This small exercise is designed to plug you into their energy and allows you easier access to the frequencies they offer. Some of these devotions you may find quite mundane, which is deliberate: the mermaids want you to get into the habit of seeing your life as one larger devotional act.

Ritual: In many respects, ritual is a form of devotional work. Its main difference is that ritual is done for a very intentional reason, and generally at a very specific time. This means ritual is not an everyday habit, nor is it something that you would be required to maintain over the long-term. It is done in addition to your daily work. Ritual enhances your devotional practice and, in many respects, gives it depth and width.

Healing: Energy runs through everything we do. It is part of how we speak, think, act, engage, react, and live. In this book, the healing exercises are connected to one of the seven major chakras, with the exception of the exercise in chapter 1, which is for your aura. These healing exercises may be meditations, but they aren't always, as they align themselves to the teachings of each water deity. These healing exercises are mainly for mental, emotional, and vibrational purposes; none of them are to heal you of serious illness. Always consult a licensed professional if you require medical or therapeutic advice.

Spellwork: In this book, the spells could have also been called prayers, for that is what they are. I have always considered spells and prayers to be identical in nature. They are each a petition, spoken out loud to a deity we cannot see, asking for a problem to be resolved or a thing to manifest in our lives. Both are generally done at an altar. I am using the world *spell* for this book; however, you can use the word *prayer* if it aligns better for you.

These exercises often lead into one another, but you do not need to do them sequentially to benefit from them. Instead, allow the energy of the mermaids to flow through you and intuitively allow this energy to guide you to which exercise you need for your current situation. You could even use this book as a daily devotional tool. Sit quietly with it in your hands, centering yourself and taking a few deep breaths in through the nose. Then, flip to any page and use the content as your guide for the day.

Personally, I am a fan of working through books like this one via bibliomancy. The bibliomancy style of reading is pretty simple to follow; it is similar to using a book for devotional work, except you also have a timer and notebook with you. It goes something like this: Focus your breath for a moment, taking long, slow breaths in through the nose and out through the mouth. Then, ask the mermaids to show you what message they have for you today. Flip through the book and open it randomly. Point somewhere on the page and read from where you finger landed for five minutes. Once your five minutes are up, pick up your notebook and start taking notes on anything that grabbed your attention. You can take this a step further by seeing if you can write an affirmation statement based on the notes you took.

There really are so many ways to play with the contents of this book and to connect with the deities that reside in the Mermaid Pantheon.

The Chakras

Chakra Figure

This is not a book about chakras. It mentions them and they are a very important part of the content, but it is not a chakra book. Yet, I could not write this book without dedicating space and time to each of the energy centers we call chakras. I have been working with, on, and through these seven major energy centers for well over a decade. They are an integral part of my life and my work. The more I work with them, the more information they seem to impart. I am beginning to feel like I will never really get to the bottom of all the things these incredible vortexes of power have to teach us.

In this book, you will see that each chakra is assigned a specific issue or concern that we explore throughout the entire chapter. This means that the chakra work in each chapter is only one part of the overall teaching for that issue or concern—this is why this is not a chakra book. I have been incredibly selective with the content I have used for this particular book. If you want a bit more information, I recommend you take a peek at my book *Tarot Healer*.

For those of you who are wondering what on earth I am babbling about, here is chakra 101. You (and all other living beings) have an electromagnetic field that surrounds your entire physical body. Throughout this field, there are spinning discs of energy known as chakras. There are thousands of them running through your field, most of them quite small. Most of these small chakras connect to the seven major chakras, which are the largest of these discs. The seven main vortexes of energy run through your field and body like little tunnels of whirling potential. These seven chakras start at the base of your spine and end at the top of your head. The seven main chakras are the root chakra, the sacral chakra, the solar plexus chakra, the heart chakra, the throat chakra, the third eye chakra, and the crown chakra; their name kinda gives away where you can find them on your body. Each of these chakras deals with specific issues and concerns, physical areas of well-being, and your spiritual journey experiences.

Root Chakra

Root Chakra

This chakra is located at the base of your spine. It is your first chakra, and it connects you to the world of physical and material things. This chakra's main job is to tether you to the physical world and make sure you survive. In the world of the Mermaid Pantheon, I have linked the root chakra to the sprite, and for this book we are focusing on the issues of connection and stability as well as what it means to move into the energy of thriving.

Sacral Chakra

Sacral Chakra

This chakra is located in your pelvis. It is your second chakra, and it deals with the emotional world, your past, and all the dreams you wish to create or birth. In this book, I have connected this chakra to the mermaid archetype of the nymph. The issues we are looking at with the sacral chakra are that of place, meaning, and how to harness your emotions for manifestation.

Solar Plexus Chakra

Solar Plexus Chakra

This chakra is located just above your belly button. It is your third chakra, and it deals with action, desire, reaction, anger, aggression, and strategy. In this book, you will find the third chakra connected to the archetype of the shapeshifter. The issues we will look at regarding this chakra will be transmutation, karmic consequences, and habitual behavior. This chakra asks you to raise your awareness about how you move and engage with the world around you.

Heart Chakra

Heart Chakra

This chakra is right in the middle of your chest, at your heart—the name is a bit of a giveaway with this energy center. This chakra is a mediator between the energies of the physical world and the energies of the vibrational world. This makes it another connection point in your energy field. The heart chakra is connected to the common mermaid and, in this book, the issues we deal with are the common issues of being human. Spoiler: being common is super magical!

Throat Chakra

Throat Chakra

Again, the name of this one gives away where you will find your fifth chakra. This energy center rules the throat, mouth, jaw, and ears. This is primarily your center of communication, permission, and consent. For this book, I have connected this energy center to the archetype of the siren. The main issues we will look at are consent, habit, and how to communicate what you truly desire. Words have power, and we are going to explore how you are using (or not using) them in this section of the book.

Third Eye Chakra

Third Eye Chakra

This chakra is located in the middle of your forehead, just above the brow line. Your sixth chakra point is considered your center of second sight. This energy center is the eye you see with when your physical eyes aren't enough. That is what this chakra is connected to: intuition, insight, prophecy, and mystical vision. I have linked this chakra to the sea witch for the purposes of this book. Issues you will deal with in this book are the future, manifesting, activating your soul sight, and being able to hold long-term dreams and goals. There is more to this chakra than meets the eye—pardon the pun.

Crown Chakra

Crown Chakra

This chakra is located at the top of your head. If you were to trace a line from this chakra all the way through your body, you would go through all the lower six chakras, making your way to the root chakra. The crown is your seventh chakra and is also a connection point in your electromagnetic field. This point connects you to the vibrational world, the one that has no form. It is where all things begin and end. This energy center is often referred to as you center of faith as it plugs you into all that you cannot identify with the five senses. This energy center is linked to the Ocean Goddess.

One of things I did not realize I had done with this book until after I had completed it was that I started this book at the crown chakra. This means you will journey down the chakra system in this book, starting at the top and working your way down to the lower chakras. I did not do this consciously; it was merely the way the content ended up rearranging itself. I guess the water goddess wanted to be your first point of contact for this book. That being said, there really is no wrong or right way to work with these seven energy centers. You can even start in the middle of this book and be just fine.

Moon Phases

I have a confession to make: I have been wanting to write a book about the moon for years. The truth is, no matter how many times I tried, I just could not get the content to work the way I wanted it to, and I *really* tried. I spent many hours, and many thousands of words, trying to get the moon content to work. But it just would not click into place—until now. Sometimes an idea takes a while to land. Many times, the parts of an idea come before the theme. Never in a million years would I have thought that the reason the moon hounded me was because it was waiting for the mermaids to make a splash in my creative consciousness. But here we are, and now you get to read about how the moon and the mermaids work together to create portals of possibility. In this book, the eight phases of the moon have been linked to members of the Mermaid Pantheon.

This book isn't really a moon book, even though each moon phase corresponds to a lunar lesson and enhances the experience you will have with the water deity. Just keep an open mind when you work through the section of this book. I have not written the moon sections from an astrological standpoint or even a witchy standpoint, as I am not a witch. I tend to deal with these sorts of things through my priestess lens, which means I have worked with the water goddess and the energy of the mermaids to write about each moon phase. That means that the content in each of these sections may or may not correspond to what you already know about the moon, or how you are currently working with the moon phases. For the sake of this book, just flow with the content the mermaids have curated for you. The mermaids and I put this book together the way we have for a reason.

New Moon: Water Goddess

New Moon

Things tend to begin where they end, and the moon is no different. It ends in the dark and starts there as well. You will start your journey with the new moon and at the feet of the water goddess. The water goddess is the mother of all who are born from the water, born from the dark. Your adventure will kick off with choosing to learn how to let go of all that led you to this point in your life; you will move forward in a new cycle and with a new way of seeing the world, through the lens of the water goddess.

Waxing Crescent: Ocean Priestess

Waxing Crescent

The first glimpse of what is to come is found here, in the waxing crescent. During this moon phase, you will learn that light is inevitable; all things eventually leave the dark behind. You are still learning and preparing for a new adventure, so who better to instruct you on this part of your moon journey than the ocean priestess. You may have started at the feet of the Goddess, but learning how to keep her light with you day after day is the task of the priestess.

First Quarter: Sea Witch

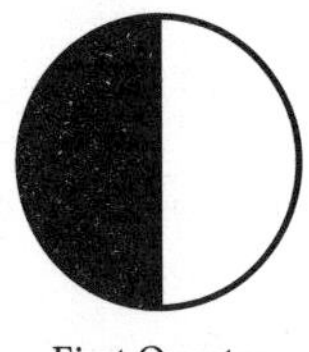
First Quarter

It is not easy to stand with one foot in the light and one still in the shadows you came from. Thank goodness you will have the council of the sea witch to assist you. The balance of boundaries is important, and we all need to make sure we know how to juggle this duality. The first quarter moon is when you look at how your light is growing and what it means to expand into the light. There will still be things you need to learn and organize during this moon phase, so do not push too hard for results just yet.

Waxing Gibbous: Siren

Waxing Gibbous

I don't know why, but this moon phase always reminds me of the Jennifer Lopez song "Let's Get Loud." Maybe that is why the siren wanted to be connected with this particular moon phase. Under this moon phase, you are becoming very exposed, and it is the right time to start letting those around you know that you have arrived. It's sort of like the invitation to a party that hasn't happened yet; preparations are being made and people need to be notified. There is a lot of communication that happens under this moon phase, so keep some warm water or hot herbal tea nearby, as you will find yourself singing along with the sounds of the siren.

Full Moon: Common Mermaid

Full Moon

The spotlight is lit: let the party begin! The full moon is all about being seen. Under this moon, there is nowhere to hide and all will be exposed. Sometimes that can be terrifying, and sometimes that can be exciting. The good news is, you won't be the only one exposed. Everyone the full moon touches will be outed. This makes the full moon a bit common, to be honest; there isn't anything special about something that happens to everybody. Luckily, you have the common mermaid as your guide for this particular moon phase. You see, sometimes common is actually exceptional, especially when you know how to feel into the vibes of the light.

Waning Gibbous: Shapeshifter

Waning Gibbous

Now that the party is over and all the expectation inside you has deflated, you will more than likely need a nap. The waning gibbous brings some relief from all the energy you spent building up to and during the full moon. With the light starting to recede, you can finally take a moment and catch your breath. This might also be a good time to slip out of your busyness; pull on your comfy self as you shapeshift from needing to get things done to letting things go. Under this moon phase, you will explore all the different versions of who you are and have been, and you'll look at who you wish to be as you move in the shadows.

Last Quarter: Nymph

Last Quarter

After all the excitement of this moon cycle, it is time to come back to yourself, to redefine your boundaries and settle into just being *you* once again. The shadows are growing and the dark is calling you home. Under this moon phase, you might find yourself torn between wanting to embrace the stillness the shadows bring and yet still not quite feeling ready to slow down. The nymph is your guide for this moon phase, and they are very connected to place, which means they have no trouble bringing you back to a more contained and limited state of being. This is necessary in order for you to sink into the healing lessons this moon phase brings with it.

Waning Crescent: Sprite

Waning Crescent

Now that you have set your boundaries and gathered your energy, you might be feeling somewhat restless—maybe even a little mischievous as the darkness wraps itself around you like a warm hug. There may be a hint of revelry and celebration in the air as you come to the end of yet another powerful lunar cycle. Sprites are playful water deities and like nothing more than to raise a cup to all they have accomplished in a cycle. As the light fades and day-to-day needs calm down, the sprites invite you to let loose and shake off any last fragments of the cycle you may be holding on to. Now is not the time to be focusing on what did not happen this lunar cycle. Instead, focus on everything that went right, fell into place, and aligned itself with your needs.

There is one last moon lesson I have saved for the very end. This is my gift to you for making it through the book. Do your best not to peek at it just yet, as it is meant to help you go deeper once you have already made your way through the content. I have left the last moon lesson at the very end because I do not want you to have any sort of bias as you make your way through the moon's lessons, because the mermaids and I would very much like you to get as much out of each moon phase as possible.

The Importance of Place

There is a part of this book that is very special. The most important part of this book—after our main stars, the mermaids—is the idea of place. Understanding of place is crucial to any and all devotional practices. You need to know where you are and how your environment shapes who you are becoming. In many respects, modern humans have moved away from devotional work around place, which is shown in our disconnection from the land, the food supply, and the environment in general. The mermaids and I hope that after you have spent some time with the contents of this book, you might start to consider the importance of place in your daily life.

Place used to be sacred to our ancestors. They understood its power and were able to harness its magic. The mermaids feel it is time to come back to this old teaching. They are not alone in this sentiment; the Fae community has been vocal about it over the last five years. I have worked and channeled the Fae for quite some time now, and the messages that have come through me (often in front of a live audience) have been about the environment and the urgency for humanity as a whole to plug back into place. They very much want us to be tapped into the messages of the natural world—a world that is struggling right now. We share our world with the Fae and the merfolk, and they need us to do our part as custodians of place. This is why each chapter gives you a new place to connect to, learn from, and commune with.

The Deep Ocean

There is a difference between the ocean you see from the shoreline and the one that you need satellites to see. The deep ocean is not somewhere the average person visits. It is for whales, cargo vessels, the odd research ship, and, more than likely, the military. Yet, the deep ocean is where most of the watery activity takes place. It is ancient, mysterious, and relatively unknown to humans. It has been dubbed "the final frontier" by many eager explorers. It holds secrets to the past that could be the key to our future.

The Bay

Most of us have our first contact with the ocean via a bay. Standing on the sand, overlooking the calmer waters cradled in the loving arms of the bay, is where most of us tend to transplant ourselves when we dream of the ocean. You may have even had your first mermaid encounter while visiting a bay. This particular body of water offers a gentle entry point to the ocean and all its magic and wonder. There is a safety to this body of water; it offers us a way to explore without fear.

The Sea

Even in the water, there are in-between places, spaces with blurry borders where the edges seem more like transitions then a hard thing to cross. The sea is one of those places. The lines are distorted here. The waters can change quickly, and you can move from one place to another without even knowing it. Balance is something one may seek in the sea, yet this might be the place it is hardest to obtain, especially when there is nothing solid to hold on to. The sea will teach you to find your footing even when there is nothing to stand on.

The Waterfall

There is something magical about a waterfall. It has the ability to stop you in your tracks. It is dramatic and has no problem being seen. The waterfall will sparkle and shine for any camera that wants to capture it, yet it won't stop or stand still. You have to engage with it as it moves and flows in perpetual motion. Waterfalls are also places of water that are not confined to the edges of the landmasses. Some of the most dramatic ones will be found inland, landlocked, demanding that *you* come to *it*. This proves the awesomeness of their magical powers.

The Shoreline

This is another in-between place. This is where the water and the land meet, dance, merge, and honor each other's boundaries. Mermaid gifts and magical ocean tools are delivered on the waves and left in the sand. Birds feed; squirrels, rabbits, and other small creators burrow in the dunes. The shoreline is a hive of activity—at least during low tide. It becomes an entirely different space during high tide, when everything is suddenly submerged and under the water's caress. This is why things often appear temporary on the shoreline: Here one minute, gone the next. What was may have been swept away. Nothing can be taken for granted here, which means lessons of temporary existence and quick decisions are often left after the water recedes.

The Lava

It might seem odd to add lava to a list of watery places. But honestly, how could I not? Lava is the fiery water that flows through the veins of the earth's core. It spreads like blood across the planet we call home. And just like the blood that pumps through our bodies, when the pressure builds, it erupts. Lava pours out of the earth and changes the landscape forever. Nothing is ever the same after the lava has cooled and hardened into its new form. Lessons of intensity, quick action, and new beginnings are wrapped up in the teachings of the place known as lava. The wisdom might burn sometimes, but at least you won't forget it. The energy here is life-changing. It will move you, guide you, and set your actions on a course that there will be no coming back from. This is exciting, terrifying, and essential to all who seek the path of healing and expansion.

The Lake

There is a place where water can be deep and large, yet contained and limited in its experience. That place would be a lake. The lake is so very different to every other watery place in this book, as the lake has nowhere to go. It is the end of the road for water. Even worse, lakes can stagnate and dry up completely. The world's lakes are in a bit of a crisis, to be honest, and climate change is forcing us to take a closer look at how important these watery places are. Lakes have their own unique ecosystems, and most of us have no idea just how important lakes are for all the beings who rely on water to live, humans included. The place known as the lake will teach you about boundaries, the magic of limitation, and the miraculous power of containment.

The Ice

In 2016, when I was first designing my tarot deck *Mermaid Tarot*, I knew ice was going to be one of the places that would be featured in the deck. This made life very interesting for my artist, especially when it came to considering how things move over ice. What I learned while doing that deck was just how wise and playful ice is. The ancients whisper their stories through the ice. There are worlds contained in the ice. There is activity all over the ancient ice shelves on our planet. And, like our lakes, they are having a moment of concern. Yet, despite the problems our current world is throwing at the ice, it stands firm, solid, unpredictable, and full of mischief. No wonder the sprites wanted to teach its lessons!

Just like the chakras and the phases of the moon, the lesson of place is very much a part of the mermaid energy that governs it. The mermaids and I ask you to keep an open mind about where we have placed the Mermaid Pantheon and what sort of environment they wished to represent. This might not be how you personally would have assigned them, but for the sake of this particular book, this is how the mermaids asked me to lay things out. By that I mean: I did not randomly dump the archetypes in an environment; they chose to be there based on the lessons, guidance, and healing they wished to bring to this book and to you, the reader.

As you move through the chapters, you will see how all these parts—the chakras, phases of the moon, and place—work together to bring you a deeper understanding of each mermaid archetype. All of these sections were written not just to complement one another, but to lead you on a journey of discovery of yourself, of your life, and of how you have been molded by the people and spaces around you. These sections are also a map of how you can move beyond where you are to grow, gain confidence and clarity, and transform yourself from the inside out.

Before You Dive All the Way In

The beginning of this book has given you a lot of information. Before you go any further and meet the mermaids awaiting you in these pages, stop for a moment and quiet your mind. Focus on your breath and place your hands on your heart. Before you flip the page and move on, let us first tune in to your mermaid heart, the one that beats in time to the merfolk. Let us sync it with the vibrational energy of your follow mermaids; they have been waiting for you, calling you from across time and space.

As you focus on your breath and the beating of your heart, cast your mind back to the very first time you heard the call of the mermaids. Was it while reading a story? Watching a movie? Or during a summer on the beach, as you scanned the waves hoping to catch a glimpse of their tails? Bring this moment into your heart and lock the memory in place. Let it beat through you and out of you: from your heart to the frequency of all those who share your mermaid soul.

Know that this book has found its way to you because of the moment that now beats inside of you. The mermaids have called this moment forth. They have conspired with time and space so they could finally have this moment with you. What a gift! Breathe, relax, and honor this moment. Thank you, mermaids. Thank you for bringing us all together at this time, in this place, right here, in this moment.

Now, let the journey continue.

one
The Water Goddess

There are times when an event, a moment, can move you so deeply and profoundly that everything in your life just makes sense. These moments seem to come out of the blue and often take us by surprise. I believe this happens for a reason, the reason being: These moments push us back into our soul flow. They stop us from drifting and plug us back into the moment, deeply grounding us into our own humanity. I had one of these moments in December 2019 just as I was preparing the proposal for this book.

"To all the artists out there, go forth into the darkness and be the light." These were the closing words to Amanda Palmer's December 2019 London concert. The concert had climaxed with Amanda's story of miscarriage, her solo moment of pain, anguish, and blood—a moment that happened alone, in a blizzard, on top of a mountain. I don't think I have ever been as deeply opened up as I was listening to that story; it concluded with Amanda singing a song from *Frozen*. Everything that happened in the last twenty minutes of that concert is the energy that flows through this chapter.

Amanda's concert was, in many respects, a memoir, walking the audience through milestone moments in her life—moments that have, in so many ways, shaped her, defined her, and carved out the woman she continues to create. She was open, transparent, raw, and deeply personal. She taught by showing, by retelling, and by creating. Just like the water goddess.

Amanda overflowed with who she is, everything that pains her, and everything that drives her to deeper compassion. I gave her a standing ovation from my then-home in Las Vegas, so many miles away. Crying, I faced my computer, which was live-streaming the concert, and yelled, "You are a f*cking goddess!" It was only when I sat down to write this chapter that I realized just how much of a water goddess moment that entire concert was.

The water goddess is about tapping into an energy that is deep, raw, and profoundly personal. This energy threatens to push you over the emotional edge. The water goddess doesn't mess around. They are not here to placate you. They want you to feel it all. They want the energy to pump through your blood, to spill out of you in a way that can't be hidden. The water goddess wants you exposed and open, because only then can their energy move through you and align you with all the power of the higher version of you, the you that vibrates all that is and ever was, the vibrational part of your being that never has been and never will be physical.

Throughout this chapter, you will be introduced to the many faces of the water goddess. You will meet them in their feminine form and their nonbinary form. You will explore the energy they work with and the moon phases they connect with. You will be asked to do ritual, to practice devotion, and to step into ceremony. You will be gifted with healing, given moments of clarity, and offered new points of perspective. All the goddess asks in return is your surrender and trust. Let go and have faith.

Mermaid Archetype: Water Goddess

Deep within the oceans of time and space is the water goddess. They are pure divine energy, pumping with raw creation magic. There is nothing this goddess can't do, be, or create. This goddess knows nothing of limits and doesn't understand human fear and doubt. If you want to stand before the goddess and learn the secrets they guard, then you have to be willing to change your lexicon. The water goddess is the most powerful archetype in the Mermaid Pantheon. This goddess sits at the top of the mystical tower, and all those who seek higher knowing come to offer whatever they can carry.

The water goddess is not a single entity; they are many, varied, and multifaceted, and they have made their way into all cultures across the human world. You may know them as:

- Amphitrite
- Brizo
- Kymopoleia
- Doris
- Ceto
- Anuket
- Boann
- Brigantia
- Ehuang
- Ganga
- Isis
- Sequana
- Sinann
- Styx
- Coventina
- Juturna
- Nerthus
- Sulis
- Oshun
- Nāmaka

But these are not the water goddess's only names and forms. Honestly, their name is not as important as the messages they have and the devotion they seek. Right now, in the current climate crisis, they want you to move beyond the labels of their past identities and instead build a new relationship with them through the water you drink, bathe in, swim in, and admire from the shoreline. This goddess is not just the water outside of you; they are also the water inside of you. The body of an adult human is up to 60 percent water.[1] How you honor and treat the water *inside* of you says a lot about how you treat and think about the water *outside* of you.

Devotional Practice

The first step in your devotional practice to the water goddess is to start seeing your body's water as sacred: something to protect, honor, heal, and keep clean. You can start by practicing the sacred act of hydration. Each glass of water you put inside your body is an act of honoring the goddess. Making sure that water is the purest it can be is an act of honoring the body of the goddess. You expect it to be pure so it does not contaminate your body or corrupt your cells. Know that by choosing clean water for your body, you are committing an act of eco-activism, for when you demand clean water for your physical vessel, you demand clean water for the planet. This simple act of drinking a glass of clean water has a ripple effect far beyond what you could possibly fathom, but the

1. Water Science School, "The Water in You: Water and the Human Body," United States Geological Survey, May 22, 2019, https://www.usgs.gov/special-topics/water-science-school/science/water-you-water-and-human-body.

water goddess knows. They are very aware that small, seemingly inconsequential acts have the most massive impact.

Take your simple act of drinking a glass of water one step further and pray over it. Bless it. Fill it with the energy of a sacred sound current. This will change the structure of the water, which in turn will change the structure inside of your physical body. Try this simple water prayer over the next several days and see how infusing water with the power of the water goddess benefits you:

Goddess of the water
Bless this glass and what it now holds
Fill this liquid with your love, light, and power
Flow through me
As rain runs over mountains
Shaping me into your will
In your service I become
As mist above to waves below
Now it is so

This brings us to the first teaching of the water goddess: You and the water are one. There is no point of separation. The shoreline is an illusion. Water stops where it wants to stop. There is nothing that keeps it in place except its own intention to be where it wants to be. Change the conditions, shift the intention, and the shoreline will disappear, eaten up by the will of the water. This is also the first lesson to higher knowledge: Creation is intention. What you intend will be. When an intention is created, conditions change. When conditions change, everything shifts. What was will no longer be. Where there was something old, something new will emerge. This is the power of the water goddess. They hold the lessons of creation in the palm of their hands and offer it up to you. Will you be brave enough to step forward and take it?

The water goddess created everything in the Mermaid Pantheon. The water goddess is where they began and where they will end. The goddess controls the cycles of the sea, the tides, the currents, and all who live under the protection of their watery world.

Moon Phases: New Moon

I have always thought that the term "new moon" was a bit of a misnomer, to be honest, because although we do eventually get a new moon at the end of this particular moon phase, I would argue that this moon phase is really a rebirthing moon. It is here that light is snuffed out and then sparked anew. There is both a sense of grief and joy attached to this moon phase, a sense of both having to be forced to watch something end and at the same time feeling a sense of relief that it is over. In this respect, the new moon offers us a paradox: It is both everything and nothing. It is where the light goes to die and the place where light is reborn. It offers no promises yet stands on the threshold of unlimited potential. This is why you may sometimes feel the pull to retreat and reflect under a new moon, whereas other times you find yourself buzzing with energy and bursting to start something new. The new moon phase is governed by the water goddess, as they understand the energy of paradox more than anyone else in the Mermaid Pantheon. In this section, you will find two rituals, one for grief and reflection and another for new beginnings and rebirth. The water goddess wants you to understand that you will intuitively know which of these to use under the new moon cycle.

If you have been experiencing a lot of endings in your life, you will probably use the grief and reflection ritual. If you have been gearing up for new projects or are about to start a new job or new chapter in your life, you will probably use the ritual for rebirth and new beginnings. We won't all be at the same place come the new moon, but we will be exactly where we're meant to be. Learning to honor where you are, under the watchful gaze of the water goddess, is important.

So, where are you? Before you dive into one of the rituals, stop for a moment and be still. Place your hand on your heart and breathe deep and slow. Call in the water goddess. (You can call them in by name if you are working with one of the deities listed at the beginning of this chapter.) Ask the goddess to show you where you are. If it is easier for you to visualize with your eyes closed, do so, but know it is not necessary.

Let the water goddess guide you through the events of your life and pinpoint where in this new moon phase you find yourself. Once you have located where you are, ask the water goddess what step you should take next. How can you best use the energy of grief, or what aligned action can you take to start creating momentum around all the newness flowing into your life? Remain still and breathe while the answers, signs, and intuitive hits bubble up. Do not force them or even try to make sense of them right now. Just allow them to come to the surface and bob around in the light.

When you feel complete, thank the water goddess and take one last deep breath. Bring yourself back to the moment, opening your eyes if they were closed and removing your hand from your heart. Take a few minutes to write down everything that showed up for you while you were connected to the water goddess. Even if something doesn't seem relevant now, you never know how important it may be tomorrow, next week, or even next month.

Now, go ahead and select ritual one or ritual two.

Ritual 1: Grief

Grief is a journey we travel when something we love transitions from our experience. For most, this happens through death. But that is only one way to lose something you love. It can be the end of a relationship, the loss of a job, or even the knowledge that it is time to move on and leave things behind you know you will miss. We all go through the stages of this journey differently and over different time frames. The water goddess knows that some like to take this journey quickly, while others prefer to take longer. The goddess understands that grief is not a race and it needs to travel at your own pace, on your own time.

Knowing where you are on your grief journey is important for this ritual, as you will be asking the new moon and the water goddess for healing energy around your current experience. Part of this identification process is claiming this grief, and I mean *really* claiming it. Feel it—all of it—deeply, sharply, and intimately. Do not try to curate your emotions when it comes to grief; this is a journey you need to take as honestly and transparently as possible. Feel your way into your point on the grief journey and know that the dark moon is covering you, sheltering your emotions, reactions, and responses as the water goddess washes away your tears and stands witness to your pain.

You can do this ritual in the bath or the shower. If you happen to live near a body of water and it is safe to swim in at night, you can do the ritual there as well; there will be separate instructions for the outdoor ritual at the end. Ultimately, you need to be somewhere you can be stripped bare and in water.

MAGICAL ITEMS

A Candle: It really doesn't matter what color you choose; make sure to also grab a lighter or matches

Lavender, Rosemary, and Rose: These can be in essential oil form (a blend of one drop rose, one drop rosemary, and two drops lavender) or as dried herbs, which you can either place in a tea bag or throw straight into your bathwater

A Short Intention, Affirmation, or Prayer: This is something to say over the water to bless it

To start your ritual, light your candle and hold your hands in prayer position while you take a few slow deep breaths. This brings your awareness to the ritual and allows you a moment to ground and center, leaving the outside world alone for the time being.

Once you feel connected to the energy of the ritual, prepare your water space. If you are taking a bath, wait till your water is almost filled before adding the oils/herbs. If you are taking a shower, consider rubbing the oils into your shampoo and use the act of washing your hair as part of your ritual, or throw your herb bag at the base of the shower and allow the heat to steam and infuse the healing power of the plants.

Once you have your oils or herbs dealt with, bless your water. Say your prayer out loud and then immerse yourself in the water. Ask the water goddess to come in and assist you in cleansing away the next layer of your grief. Remember, this is not about getting rid of your grief; this is about lovingly and gently restoring yourself through the grieving process.

You may feel the presence of the goddess with you, or you may just have a knowing that you are doing some deeper work. Stay in the water as long as you feel guided to. Trust your gut about when to remove yourself from the water. It will be different for everyone. Some will require longer in the blessed waters of the goddess than others. Stay open; trust and flow with the energy the goddess is pumping through the water. Once you get out of the water, stand beside the bath or shower and say "I now release you so I can fill with light" as you watch the water go down the drain.

Close your ritual by putting your hands back into prayer position, thanking the goddess, and blowing out the candle. If you feel inclined, you can journal about the ritual and anything that came up with you were partaking in it.

If you have decided to do this ritual in a lake or river, or even down by the ocean, mix your essential oils with some coconut oil to use after you come out of the water. You won't need a candle if you do this ritual outside. (Remember, only do this in open water if it is safe to do so. If not, your bathroom works just fine.) Stand at the water's edge and say your intention/affirmation/prayer. Call the goddess, dunk yourself, and come back to shore when they prompt you to. As you stand back on the shore, say, "I now release you so I can fill with light." Then, rub the coconut oil mixture into your skin.

Ritual 2: Rebirthing Tea Ritual

No human walking this earth escapes the rebirthing process. We do it every morning we wake up, leaving the day before behind while we slept and birthing into a new day. We do it when we end a cycle or relationship in our life. A rebirth can happen when we leave an old job, outgrow a situation or experience, or even when we shift beliefs and do healing work. In many respects, we flow in and out of rebirthing energy on a consistent basis. Even though this particular ritual is for the new moon, you can bring this new moon energy and ritual into your life when any of the above happens. Just know that the energy around this ritual is amplified when paired with an actual new moon cycle.

MAGICAL ITEMS

A Candle: It really doesn't matter what color or size; when in doubt, go for a white tea light

The Rind of an Orange and a Lemon, Along with a Few Leaves of Fresh Mint: Place the citrus rinds and the mint leaves in a tea bag or just throw them straight into a teapot infuser

A Kettle: You'll use this to boil water

A Short Intention, Affirmation, or Prayer: This is something to say over the water to bless it

Fill your kettle and place it on the stove to boil or, if it's an electric kettle, flick its switch and let it do its thing. Place your tea bag of citrus rinds and mint leaves in a cup or prepare your teapot infuser. Place your hands in prayer position and take a couple of slow deep, grounding breaths. Call in the water goddess and ask them to step forth and participate in your rebirthing tea ritual. Once your water boils, pour it into your cup or teapot and allow it to infuse for four or five minutes.

As the tea infuses, say your intention/affirmation/prayer over the tea. Ask the water goddess to bless and infuse the tea with the vibrational energy of your words.

Once the tea has steeped, drink it. When you come to the end of the cup or teapot, thank the water goddess. Take the rinds and mint leaves into your yard and place them under a tree. If you don't have a tree at home, find one at a local park or even at a friend's home.

The ritual is complete. You can now move forward knowing your growth and expansion have been blessed by the water goddess.

Energetic Alignment: Aura

In many ways, the aura could be considered the eighth chakra, even though that is not what it is. In the Kundalini yoga tradition, the aura is number seven of the ten bodies they work with to increase health and happiness amongst their students.[2] The aura, or auric body, is not one that a lot of people outside of energy work or yoga know too much about. But as society moves further and further into the age of Aquarius, I do believe we will start to hear conversations about the health and well-being of one's aura just as often as we hear about the health and well-being of one's skin, joints, or organs.

---

2. "The Ten Bodies," 3HO, accessed April 29, 2022, https://www.3ho.org/article/the-ten-bodies/.

For those who are wondering, the age of Aquarius is one of the astrological ages. Astrologers use astrological ages to calculate where we are in the human journey. Some say we are already in the age of Aquarius; some argue we are just getting ready to moving into it. Either way, it is very much influencing the timeline we all currently live in. As yoga studios continue to sprout up like new age coffee shops, the way we talk about our bodies and state of well-being will ultimately change. Lucky for you, the water goddess is here to guide you through this new form of healing.

So, what exactly is the aura, and how does it work in regard to healing work, health, happiness, and life overall? Think of the aura as a giant storage chip, much like the SD cards in cell phones or cameras. Just like these small cards, the aura has limited space and will stop saving your data once it has reached capacity. The downside is, we have no idea what that capacity is, which is why those in the know are constantly cleaning out their aura, getting rid of things they no longer need and making room for new things. How good you are at cleaning out things you don't need? Seriously, when was the last time you cleaned out your downloads folder or your phone? I'll be the first to admit, I am pretty bad at it and have to set reminders to do it. I also have to set reminders to clean out my aura. If you are like me and cleaning things out is not something you think about, then I suggest you get in the habit of setting yourself a weekly reminder to clean out your aura!

The reason we want to keep our aura as clear as possible is that it is the only way to attract new things in your life. Yes, you read that right, your aura is your attractor factor. It is a tractor beam from you to the Universe. Whatever energy coding you have in your aura is the frequency you will align with when you try to manifest, and if you have never updated that coding, your aura is singing a very old and outdated love song to the Universe. Your aura has been singing its song since the moment you were born: you are a creator, you were born a creator, and you and your aura have been co-creating for your whole life. This piece of you that is a natural born creator—the piece that is always tapped into your true power—is the piece of you that is connected to the water goddess. And the goddess is the one who will assist you in cleaning, clearing, and re-coding your aura. Once you understand how powerful your aura truly is, you will want to fine tune it, clear it, and re-code it as often as possible. With the water goddess by your side, you will start to see this part of your vibrational being as your friend, ally, and partner.

Aura Colors

Before we begin, I must tell you, I am not an aura reader. I don't work specifically with auras. That is actually my wife's area of expertise, so everything I know about auras, I pretty much learned from her. She was an aura reader for close to ten years, so her knowledge about aura colors and how the aura works is quite advanced. What I am giving you here is a very basic understanding of the aura, its colors, and their meanings.

Violet: This is the color of intuition and tends to reveal psychic abilities

Green: This could indicate you are in a state of healing, whether it that is physical or emotional

Yellow: This color is about joy; you are allowing it to ebb and flow in your life and communicating that joy with those around you

Blue: This is the color of communication and is extremely prevalent for creative people, especially writers, educators, and speakers

Red: This tends to indicate underlying anger; the stronger the red, the more intense the feelings of anger and resentment are

Orange: Tends to show up for those in a creative cycle or who are getting ready to birth something creative in their lives

Gold: The color of spiritual consciousness; this color can show up when you are walking a deeper spiritual path

White: Can indicate expansion or excitement about being on the brink of something new

Magenta: You are working with ideas, thoughts, and emotions that may be out of the norm; people who are on the edge of innovation will see a lot of this color in their aura

In the following exercise, you might notice the color of your aura, or you might even notice your aura's color shift or change as you move through the meditation.

Healing Exercise

In this exercise, you will learn how to cleanse and clear your aura so you can start aligning it with the things you really want instead of singing the tired song of your past.

For this healing exercise, select a water goddess from the list at the beginning of this chapter. Find one that you feel safe and comfortable bringing into your space. This is important, as you need to be able to trust the goddess when they present themselves. If you do not, you will automatically resist their healing energy and contract from all the possibilities they can bring to your life.

You will need something to cleanse your space with. You can burn some sage or palo santo, or you can use an essential oil spray. Use your herb bundles or cleansing spray around your entire house if possible; at the very least, cleanse the room you are going to be doing this exercise in. Open your windows so old, stale energy can be moved out of your space and sent back to the air goddess. If it is not too hot or windy, you can leave your windows open until you have finished with this exercise. I like to keep my windows open during healing work so the energy can find its way out of my house. However, you may wish to only open them for a couple of minutes after you've finished cleansing your space. Whatever works for you.

Once your space has been cleansed, find somewhere comfortable. Sit down, lie down, or get into your favorite yoga pose. Take a few deep, slow breaths as you focus on the here and now. Feel the breath as it moves into your body. Let yourself connect the breath to the body.

When you feel centered, imagine a circle of white light that goes around your entire body. See this thin white light like a halo around your whole body. Don't worry too much if you can't see it clearly or even if your circle of white light seems to have gaps. Trust that you can focus your attention on your auric field. Now see if you can expand or push that white circle of light out, making it bigger. See if you can double it in size, then bring it back to its original size.

Take another slow, deep breath. This time, push that white light as far as you possibly can and hold it there. Call in your water goddess and ask them to wash and cleanse your auric field. All you have to do is keep your aura expanded while the goddess works their cleansing magic. Just breathe, keeping the breath slow and deep. Do your best to hold your auric field out until the water goddess indicates the work is complete. Once the goddess is done, see if you notice any changes in your aura.

Did it change color?

Is it clearer now?

Have the gaps been filled back in?

Now, very slowly, start to contract your aura back to where you started. With each gentle breath, bring your aura closer to your body. Notice how it feels now that it is closer to your physical body again. Keep the breath slow and deep as you bring your awareness back to the room, back to your body, and back to the present moment.

If you feel moved to, journal about your experience and write out any messages your goddess delivered as they worked on the energy in your aura. When you are all done, cleanse your space again and get on with the rest of your day or night.

This simple aura healing can be done as often as you feel you need it. You can't over-clean your auric field; it's just not possible.

Place of Power: Deep Ocean

There is nowhere on the planet like the deep ocean. It is one of the last remaining frontiers we have yet to truly explore. Its depths are so vast that without some serious diving equipment, most humans can only go sixty feet down; the limits can be pushed up to 130 or 1,000 feet if you have the right gear and don't plan on being down at that depth for very long.[3] To say humans are somewhat shallow might be an understatement!

Then, of course, there is the darkness, vast and seemingly never-ending. For the water goddess, this is their underworld; this is their place of descent. Stories of descent permeate goddess stories the world over, as they are powerful examples of what it means to survive, be reborn, and harness the dark for transformation and power. The descent is when we transcend the many layers of who we believe we are and release everything that keeps us from the great mysteries. The deeper you go and the darker it becomes, the greater your chance of finding the light of wisdom.

Within mystery traditions, the descent of the goddess is often marked by moving through the seven gateways: the physical plane, the elemental plane, the astral plane, the mental plane, the spiritual plane, the divine plane, and the ultimate plane. To pass through each of these gateways, the goddess must give an offering, something that is deeply personal and something that must be let go of in order to walk through the gateway. This is a devotional act. It shows the goddess's willingness to step out of what they think they know and stand at the threshold of what they don't know. The offering is a form of humble initiation. The deep ocean asks you for the same: an offering for your descent into its waters of wisdom. So, what are you willing to give?

---

3. "How Deep Can a Human Dive with Scuba Gear?" Deep Blue Diving, accessed March 3, 2022, https://www.deepbluediving.org/maximum-depth-with-gear/.

Here in the deep ocean, you must offer something personal that you don't expect to have returned. There is always a chance the waves could wash it back up to shore, but ideally, it needs to be something you release and let go of. Keep in mind that you won't actually go out to the middle of the ocean to give these things to the water.

Your offering could be a physical act, one where you give something that you no longer need. Perhaps it is something that has sentimental value but sits in the dark corner of your storage closet, or it could be photos of past loves that you clung to because you decided that particular ex played a part in your story, but now the goddess asks to strip you of this story. Maybe your offering is emotional in nature and you are willing to hand over grief, anger, or pain to the deep ocean so it can be transformed. Your offering could even be mental; you could offer your negative thought patterns and let them dissolve with the pull of the undertow. There are many ways to give your offering to the deep ocean.

Spellwork

The act of offering here will be done via devotional ritual. To do this, gather the things you are offering or giving away. If you are doing a physical offering, grab what you intend to release from your life. You can give it to charity, throw it in the trash, or even burn it. For thoughts or emotions, write these out and use the paper you have written them on as your physical offering; to honor the water goddess, you will work to release these things inside of you, breaking this habitual pattern once and for all.

The act of offering does not need to be done at an altar. It can be done just by invoking the water goddess's name. You can simply say, "I give this offering in the name of [the water goddess]."

If you want a more ritualized approach, set up an altar to the water goddess and place your offerings on it. Light a black candle and recite a small prayer, something along the lines of:

Dark goddess of the water
I offer you this part of me
A piece of who I used to be
Lay it at your threshold
To walk through your gate
Initiate me in your mysteries
Clean me and set me free
I give this to you, mother of the deep ocean
Hear my request
As it is said, so shall it be

If possible, leave your candle burning. If that's not possible, do a small blessing of the light before you snuff it out.

If you feel inclined, journal about how you feel after the offering has been done. You may feel lighter, more energized, or even more inspired. Journaling will allow you to capitalize on the new energy the water goddess has bought into your life. Just stay open, humble, and willing to receive.

This ends your offering to the deep ocean. Now that you have made your offering the goddess, they will expect to receive it, and they have no problem coming to collect what is owed.

Mermaid Connection Exercise: Journaling with the Water Goddess

You have done a lot of work in this chapter. You have done healing work by moving energy around your aura. You have rebirthed under the new moon and participated in a devotional ritual. This feels like a good time to crack open your journal and reflect on what you have learned about yourself while working with the water goddess.

- Which water goddess did you feel a connection to, and what gift or lesson did they bring you?
- What energy did you feel the most under the new moon's influence, grief or rebirth? What was it about this energy that felt powerful and profound?
- When you worked with your aura, how did it make you feel?
- What was your biggest "aha moment" while working through this chapter, and why is it important to where you are in your life right now?
- How will you bring the energies of this chapter into your daily life more fully?

Think of these prompts as a way to start the reflecting process. Do not feel limited by these questions; allow your answers to open up more discussion. Let your thoughts flow freely. There is magic in letting the words spill onto the page. Once you feel complete, move on to the cartomancy work.

Cartomancy: The Empress

The Empress

The energy of the water goddess is deeply connected to the Empress card in a tarot deck. This card is connected to the planet Venus and goddesses of love and creation. If you are not a tarot person, you can use an oracle deck that aligns to your water goddess for the following exercise.

This is a simple technique to use when you want to receive guidance from the water goddess. Place the Empress card or an aligned oracle card faceup in front of you. This is your anchor card, also known as your significator; it grounds the energy of your inquiry and focuses it squarely on the Empress. Pick up the rest of your deck and shuffle. While you shuffle, think of a question and bring it into your mind's eye. Some sample questions are:

- What is the best action for me to take today?
- What emotions should I avoid attaching to today?
- What new idea is worth exploring today?
- How can I connect more deeply with you today?

You can either pull a card for each of these questions, or you can just pull one card to answer a specific question. You can also write your own questions for the water goddess if you feel inclined to do so.

This wraps up your time with the water goddess. The mermaids and I recommend taking a small break before you dive into the next chapter to allow yourself some integration time. You have done a lot of work, even if it doesn't feel like it, so be kind and gentle to yourself. When you are ready, the mermaids and I shall see you on the next page.

two
The Ocean Priestess

There are moments in life that pull us under and drag us out of our comfort zone, far from the shore of what we know and what we take for granted. Life has a way of taking us to places we feel vulnerable, untethered, and afraid, especially when it is time to grow, expand, and break free from destructive life patterns. For me personally, this happens every seven years, as I can almost pinpoint the moment when I will get swept away from everything I have known and carried off somewhere I have to relearn everything.

This very thing happened as I was doing the mapping for this book. My wife and I had given away everything we owned, packed our lives into two suitcases, and were preparing to move to a new country when all of a sudden, we were hit with a global pandemic. Needless to say, we were not the only ones thrown into the ocean. Like many, our plans unraveled before our very eyes as the world started to close its doors and bunker down for months unknown.

Having nowhere to live, we ended up in the spare room of a friend's house and, like the rest of the world, we did our best to wait it out. However, life—much like the ocean—has a time limit on being able to wait things out. You can't stay where you are indefinitely, or at some point you will end up in an even worse situation. The open ocean is a dangerous place: Conditions change without warning. It is filled with predators. Undertows will pull you under and hold you in their grasp. Decisions will need to be made. A course will need to be charted, and you will eventually have to move. Just like my wife and I ended up having to. We decided that the world might need some recovery time, so we found our own place and carried on with rebuilding yet again. All things eventually make their way back to shore. Solid ground will return, even if you find yourself wobbly and somewhat disoriented.

Despite everything, the ocean is highly spiritual in nature. It is like a baptism. Walking into the water is an opportunity to be reborn and rebuilt, then birthed back onto the shore. When we wash up on land, we are not the same person we were when we got carried out by the waves. We have been changed in ways we won't truly know until we have reoriented to being back on land. In this respect, when we leave the ocean we are straddling two worlds, standing at the gateway of both. This is where the ocean priestess lives: straddling worlds. One leg is in the deep, vast ocean of spiritual possibilities, and one leg is firmly on the land of mundane physical existence.

In this chapter, you will see how the ocean can bring you closer to your physical and spiritual self. This chapter will teach you how to tap into the magic the bay provides and the protection it offers in the loving embrace of the priestess's arms.

Mermaid Archetype: Ocean Priestess

It would be a mistake to look for this priestess based on costume alone, for you will not find them. They are not going to look the way you think they should. They will elude your preconceived ideas and dance right under your nose without you even giving them a second thought. You see, the ocean priestess does not take themselves that seriously. They take their sacred work seriously, but not their physical expression. In this way, the ocean priestess is a bit of a trickster, and you would be excused for mistaking them for some other mermaid. The ocean priestess does this on purpose to teach you a very important lesson: power never looks the way you expect it to. Yet, humans chase the illusion of power all the time.

Only those who understand the signs of devotion will be able to spot the ocean priestess, for time floats away in their presence. Everyday tasks fascinate them, and they will be deeply inspired by the mundane. Why? Because the essence of the Goddess is in all things, and it is the job of the priestess to honor the Goddess in all her forms, to tend to her essence, and to learn from the Goddess in the simplest of ways. The most powerful ocean priestess will profoundly change you while doing nothing at all.

To know the ocean priestess is to be one with your own personal potential. To step into the shoes of the ocean priestess means to see the world through a transformational lens, one where the everyday becomes the luxury you strive for, and where a life lived with care, compassion, and kindness creates daily miracles. Stepping into the shoes of the ocean priestess means knowing how to slow down to speed up, and it also means knowing how to let go of what you want in order to have everything your heart desires. To live the life of the ocean priestess means to see all things in your life as a blessing, because everything in life came from the Goddess to move you, expand you, and keep you on your soul's path.

The ocean priestess knows there are no bad days or good days—there are just days filled with the energy of the Goddess. Life is the temple and the ocean priestess worships at its altar. If you are willing, the ocean priestess can show you how to become more connected to your daily life through the Goddess, devotion, and detachment. Just know, this is not for everyone. We are not all in the same place and space in our lives. Some are not ready to drop the quest for illusionary power; others are not willing to see all aspects of the lives they have lived as divine blessings. This path cannot be forced. You must come to it—come to the priestess—only when you are ready, certain, and able. The ocean priestess will not judge you. Instead, they will sit and wait, working on you from afar through the love they experience from the Goddess.

So, who is the ocean priestess? The ocean priestess is the head of spiritual devotion in the Mermaid Pantheon. They are the spiritual advisor to humans and mermaids alike. They maintain places of worship and show others how to pray, give thanks, and honor the Goddess. The ocean priestess can also be a seer and oracle, for they are connected to the unlimited field of potential that we are calling the Goddess. (You may call it God, the Universe, or even the Divine.) When you seek out the ocean priestess, do so because you want to bring more spiritual and devotional energy into your daily life. You may also wish to ask for guidance about your path, purpose, and soul potential.

Devotional Practice

When you are ready—and only then—start your devotional practice to the ocean priestess by seeing your daily mundane tasks as devotional practices. My biggest act of devotion to the ocean priestess is laundry. In my opinion, honoring our various costumes and coverings is a sacred act. I take laundry very seriously, unlike my wife—she deals with it like a drunk raccoon on a midnight bender. I think everything about the process of washing, drying, folding, and putting away clothes is a devotional act. Every time my wife opens the dresser or walks into the closet, she says she feels loved, cared for, and respected. That's a lot of emotion caused by laundry, but that's the power of true devotional work. Devotional work can be the simplest of tasks, but it will still have life-changing consequences.

So, what is your mundane devotional task? What is the one thing that you know you are completely present for?

Select one task and make it your sacred ocean priestess work for the next week. Each time you perform this task, make sure you are fully present, engaged, and connected to the water goddess. You may want to speak these words out loud before you begin:

Goddess, I honor you through this
My ocean priestess task

Get into the habit of grounding in the sacred energy of the devotional act. Much like the ocean priestess herself, you will have one foot in the spiritual world and one foot in the physical. Remember that no task is too small, and the tasks do not have to involve water. Your devotional task could be collecting the mail, doing the dishes, mopping the floor, brushing your teeth, washing your face, or even making the bed. These are all wonderful ways to slip into your ocean priestess role. The real energy of the ocean is to go deep. Be all in. Submerge yourself in your devotional work.

Once your week is up, see how this practice worked for you. Document your findings. Perhaps this will become a lifelong devotional practice, or maybe you will keep searching until the right one comes your way. When it comes to working with this energy, there is no wrong or right way—there is only *do*, *be*, and *act*.

Moon Phases: Waxing Crescent

The waxing crescent is shaped much like the bay; it has those loving arms that seem to circle the vast darkness of the unlit moon as it is once again reborn. Thin arms of light start to spread out over the moon's surface. These arms are a reminder, one that says "The light will always return and the darkness is fleeting." The waxing crescent is faith in light form. It is a force that will grow stronger the longer it is allowed to shine. For me, the waxing crescent is the promise of a wish bursting forth and the first signs that it is being fulfilled. We planted this wish under the darkness of the new moon, and here we start to see it shine. It may be small, but it is mighty.

The light, in many respects, is coming back to the world of physical things. The moon is bringing itself out of the womb of space and reforming itself. The arms of light that wrap around it are the arms of the midwife, the light of the priestess, for the priestess is the one who brings the energy of the Goddess into the light.

I was born under this particular moon phase, and funnily enough, I always feel like I am emerging during a waxing crescent—never quite exposed, but never truly hidden either. There is something magical about emerging, birthing, and getting another chance to start again. Perhaps that is why I am not afraid to let everything go and start again, because I was born under the promise of what is to come. I was born with the ocean priestess as my midwife, and I know this means that only things that fill me up will wash over my life. I think being born under this moon also explains my introverted personality. I like the dark, I like playing in the shadows, and I am forever the wallflower in a room of people competing to be seen. If you are born under this moon, perhaps you feel the same—or maybe you are like my wife, who was also born under this moon phase is constantly chasing the light, wanting more and more of it. But even she eventually needs her time in the dark, in the quiet, away from all prying eyes. The push and pull of wanting to emerge and wanting to retreat is strong during this moon phase.

Ritual: Emerging from the Dark

In many ways, we go through a waxing moon phase every single day when we first wake up. Every morning, you (like most people on the planet) emerge from a night's rest. There is a moment just before getting out of bed that is an exact vibrational match to this particular moon phase. While slowly becoming aware of your awakened state, you lay wrapped in the arms of your lovely blankets, supported by your pillow. These are the arms of the ocean priestess, holding you in the bay of your bed.

This state, which only lasts for a very brief moment, is the perfect time to do an emerging ritual. I do this ritual most mornings. I'll be honest, sometimes I miss my timing on this and have to get up to empty my old bladder. So, do not worry if you don't do this ritual every morning. Doing it when you remember is just fine!

The morning emerging ritual is very simple. While you are snuggled deep in your bed, keep your eyes closed. Start talking to yourself (inside your head please; other people may still be sleeping) about the day you want to have. Start with how you want to feel today. I often start with the statement "Today I am going to feel productive, calm, and joyful." Then, start thinking about how you are going to feel while doing your daily tasks and engaging with the people around you. Think about how you will feel when you are getting ready for bed that night. Once you are done, finish with the words "And so it is," then get out of bed and start your day.

This emergence ritual is all about how you feel, not about what you will do. If you find yourself drifting off or listing items on your to-do list, stop, take a breath, and bring yourself back to how you want to feel throughout the day.

When I do remember to do this emerging morning ritual, my day truly does run smoother. I find I have far more energy and I do not seem to lose time or miss tasks. This is because I am able to maintain and sustain my emotional body throughout the day. You will be amazed at what a difference this ritual can make!

Energetic Alignment: Crown Chakra

I feel like every time I sit down to write about the crown chakra, I have something different to say about it. Perhaps that is because this chakra is constantly upgrading. It changes its programming every time we shift our awareness and activate a new level of consciousness, which means each time I sit down to write about the chakras, I find myself imparting new information and new energetic technologies. Not that there is anything special about my levels of consciousness; like everyone, I am a work in progress. For me, this work is constant, and my practice is divinely imperfect. So, let me share what I am learning through my relationship with my crown chakra as I write this particular book.

In my book *Tarot Healer*, I talked about how the crown chakra is a connection point, one that plugs us into the higher self, the divine part of who we are that never experiences physical form. Since then, I've continued to learn how that connection can be amplified as we heal, clear, and do our daily spiritual practice. Now, I'm not talking about your connection getting stronger, although that is also a lovely side effect; I am talking about it getting wider, opening you to other aspects of the vastness that you never had access to before.

I am going to qualify what I am about to say by telling you that I have been channeling since 2009; I started channeling in public in 2010. This means my crown connection has been pretty strong for a while. But even though I had this strong connection, I wasn't really doing much with it. In many respects, I had taken it for granted. Then something happened while I was writing *Tarot Priestess*, something that completely changed how I now view this particular chakra: I stopped trying to guide it. I let go. I completely surrendered to my connection and sank into a vastness that was so immense I could have lost myself quite happily. It was as if the Goddess released me the moment I dropped my need to be in control. A power ran through my body like I was hit by lightning, and then there was nothing. Everything was gone, including me. It was one of the most beautiful experiences I have had thus far. I had just set up my altar at the time; I hadn't even lit my candle or said my morning prayer. I just heard a voice that said "Stop," and I did, and everything changed.

So, what really happened? Faith. Faith happened.

At that moment, I was one with faith. There was no separation between faith and me. We merged into one energy and *boom*! Together we were hurtled into the unknown. Now, I am not saying that this is something you should try at home, or even by yourself. In fact, opening your crown chakra should be done with the help of a trained teacher—someone who knows how to come get you if you do happen to get lost in the vastness. What I want you to take away from this section is how to deepen your faith and heal your trust issues with the divine. One of the biggest issues of limitation at the crown is trust; more specifically, trust in something more powerful than your physical self and ego can comprehend.

Let's bring this back to channeling. When I used to go to public events, one of the most common things I heard from people was that they did not trust the energy coming in through their crown chakra. They wanted to do what I did, but they couldn't bring themselves to open up that line of communication with something they could not see, touch, or be sure was real and safe.

The ocean priestess trusts their connection. The ocean priestess trusts their power and the capacity of their crown chakra. In many respects, the ocean priestess has spent a large part of their life healing their trust issues, and now it is your turn.

Healing Exercise

For this exercise, we're going to connect the crown chakra and the heart chakra to heal your crown chakra trust issues. One of the best ways to do this is to infuse the crown chakra with the energies of love, kindness, and compassion that pump freely through the heart chakra.

Go ahead and get comfortable. You can lie down, sit in a comfy chair, or settle into a yoga pose that you find relaxing. Take a deep breath in through the nose and as you do, drop the shoulders, relax the jaw, and exhale through the mouth. Take another deep breath in through the nose and out through the mouth, dropping the shoulders and relaxing the jaw. One more time: deep breath in through the nose, relax the shoulders, unclench the jaw, and exhale through the mouth.

Place your right hand about an inch above your heart chakra in the middle of your chest. Take your left hand and hold it an inch above the top of your head. It's important that you don't have your hands touching the body, as you are doing clearing and connecting work within the chakra points and you want to do it within the energetic body, not the physical body. That's why I've asked you to raise your hands about an inch above each chakra.

Once you have your hands in place, go ahead and close your eyes. Take a deep breath in through the nose and a relaxing breath out through the mouth. We're going to switch our breathing now, and you're going to breathe to the count of five.

Inhale one, two, three, four, five. Exhale one, two, three, four, five.

Inhale one, two, three, four, five. Exhale one, two, three, four, five.

Inhale one, two, three, four, five. Exhale one, two, three, four, five, and relax. Drop the hands, regulate the breathing, and keep the eyes closed. Shake out the arms a little bit and give yourself a small break.

When you're ready to begin the next round, place the right hand back over the heart chakra, about an inch away from the body, and place the left hand back on top of the crown chakra, making sure not to touch the head.

Inhale one, two, three, four, five. Exhale one, two, three, four, five.

Inhale one, two, three, four, five. Exhale one, two, three, four, five.

Inhale one, two, three, four, five. Exhale one, two, three, four, five. Drop the hands and shake them out. Relax the shoulders, regulate the breathing, and keep the eyes closed.

Now you're going to switch hands. Rest the left hand just above the heart chakra and the right hand at the top of the crown chakra. Again, don't touch the body. Breathe normally. This time, you're going to bring in a repetitive mantra. Say this mantra inside your head: *I trust, I release, I receive. I trust, I release, I receive.* Keep that mantra going for between thirty seconds and two minutes. Remember to breathe deep as you repeat the mantra.

When time is up, remove the hands, relax the arms, roll the shoulders, wiggle the fingers, and that's it. You are complete!

You can repeat this simple process of heart-crown coherence anytime you experience self-doubt, second-guess yourself, or just need to rebuild the confident connection between kindness and your ability to tap into something that's bigger than your ego can comprehend.

Place of Power: Bay

I have a deep and intimate connection to the part of the ocean called the bay. For years I swam in Port Phillip Bay on the southern coast of Australia. That was my happy place. There were times of the year when the water would be so still and calm that it looked like a magical mill pond. Experiencing one of those evenings under the largest full moon of the year made me believe in miracles.

I have always felt safe and protected inside the caressing arms of the bay. It was as if the ocean mother herself cradled me in a way no one in my life ever could. It wasn't until years later I found out that Port Phillip Bay is filled with sharks. In all the years I swam in that water, often at night and in the dark, I never once encountered any sharks. But then again, the bay was my sanctuary, my safe space; no harm was ever going to come to me there.

The next bay to have a major influence over my life was San Francisco Bay. One of my dear friends had an apartment in Point Richmond overlooking the bay. Each morning the sun rose on San Francisco, bathing it in golden light. Nursing a freshly brewed coffee while I wrote and watched the sunrise was like a dream come true. My *Animal Totem Tarot* was created in the marina right across the street from my friend's apartment; the Two of Wands card in that deck is my homage to that bay. It will come as no surprise that the guidebook for my *Mermaid Tarot* was also written there. What can I say—I am an ocean priestess and the bay is my place of creative power. It truly is the joke of the Universe that I live in the damn desert!

A bay is a body of water that flows into a curve in the land. It is not too big (that would be a gulf) and it's not too small (that would be a cove); it is just right. The water inside the bay is calmer than the water of the open ocean. There's a slim chance of large waves, so the bay is more swimmer-friendly, to a certain point. On the bay you will find lots of boats, generally sailboats, which are just lovely to watch on a clear day as they dance across the water. Bays are also places where you will find ports, where goods and services are imported and exported. Because of this, bays are generally busy places. There is movement, hustle, and a vibrant energy to them, especially during the day. In the evenings, however, they become still, quiet, and, dare I say it, magical!

In many respects, bays come to life when the light emerges. Fishermen tend to head out as the sun comes up. Boats come into harbor to dock in the mornings. Ferry and transportation vessels kick up service once the light settles on the arms of the bay. It is this emergence of light—the momentum created by the morning light—that we are going to focus on for our spellwork. In many respects, this spell ties into the ritual you did in the devotional section of this chapter. And if you feel inclined to do so, you can do this spell to activate the intention you set before your feet hit the floor in the morning.

Spellwork

If you are going to merge this spell with this chapter's morning ritual, I highly recommend you write down your intention statement so you can use it to anchor your spell. If you want to do this without the morning ritual (which is perfectly fine), then you are going to need to write an intention that gives your emerging energy a target. Spells work better when they have a direct bullseye to focus on. If you want to use this spell under the waxing crescent moon rather than in the morning, think about what you want to emerge during that particular moon phase. What is being birthed out of the light that is going to drive movement and momentum?

MAGICAL ITEMS

A Candle: I recommend using an orange candle to clear the path and remove any blocks or excuses, preferable a small spell candle; white will do if you can't find orange

Some Orange Peel or Wild Orange Essential Oil: This promotes movement and attraction

A Pocket-Size Tiger's Eye Crystal: This helps keep the mind clear and focused on moving toward your intentional outcome

A Small Glass of Water: You could also use a mug

To start your spell, take the orange peel or the wild orange essential oil and rub it on your candle. Once you have finished anointing your candle, place your orange peel in a glass of water, or add five drops of wild orange essential oil to a glass of water.

Take your fingers and dip them into the water, then dab the water on your wrists, heart chakra, and third eye chakra. As you do, repeat the following: "I call forth the power of the ocean priestess to infuse this candle to be my guiding light throughout the day."

Put your candle in a holder and light it. Pick up your tiger's eye and repeat the following spell:

Ocean priestess coming to me
Bring forth the energy of the bay

The light of the emerging moon
Hold me safely as I stake my claim
Ground me yet let me flow
Point me in the direction I am meant to go
I give you this, my daily prayer
My intention do you hear
[Speak your intention statement aloud]
And so it is

If it is safe to do so, leave your candle burning. If it is not, blow it out and say, "As the smoke rises, so does my intention, letting me know the ocean priestess hears me." Keep your tiger's eye in your pocket, on your altar, or even on your desk. It is your talisman, your connection to your intention. As for the glass of water, if you have a back garden you can pour the water under your favorite tree or shrub. No garden, no problem! You can add the water to a potted plant or pour it down the sink.

Now that your spell is done and you have given your intention to the ocean priestess, go about your daily business. Be open to signs from the priestess and honor them when you become aware of blessings and opportunities, as these are physical manifestations of the priestess's direct reply to your prayer/spell/petition.

If you do this spell as part of your morning routine, I highly recommend you have a small altar set up for this if it is going to be an ongoing practice. This adds an extra layer of devotion to the spellwork, not to mention it imprints this as a magical habit.

Mermaid Connection Exercise: Journaling with the Ocean Priestess

The role of the ocean priestess is one of devotion. The priestess works in service to the Goddess. All of the priestess's acts are a way of honoring the divine nature of existence. Now that you have had a chance to spend time with the ocean priestess, it is time to see how things are starting to grow in your day-to-day life. The waxing crescent is moving energy forward, allowing the light within you to grow. You are opening your connection and trusting the water goddess through your devotional acts. The safety of the bay holds you in its arms as you grow more confident in your power. Momentum is upon you, even if you are still emerging from the dark. Now is a good time to crack open your journal and reflect on what you have learned about yourself over the course of working with the ocean priestess.

- How can I bring more devotional practices into my day?
- Where do I need to be more intentional with my work?
- How can I be of service to those in my community today?
- Where can I trust more and doubt less?
- What places in my life make me feel connected and supported?

Think of these prompts as a ritual, opening up the communication process between you and the ocean priestess. Do not feel limited by these questions; allow your answers to open up more discussion. Let your thoughts flow freely. There is magic in letting the words spill onto the page. Once you feel complete, move on to the cartomancy work.

Cartomancy: The High Priestess

The High Priestess

The energy of the ocean priestess is identical to the High Priestess card in a tarot deck. This is the card of ritual, ceremony, and having one foot in the physical world and one in the realm of spirit. There is deep wisdom and knowledge associated with this card and the archetypal energy of the priestess. If you are not a tarot person, you can use an oracle deck that has a priestess on it; there are several oracle decks that give a nod to the priestess and the keeper of sacred and devotional acts. It should not be hard to find one in your deck collection.

Place the High Priestess card or an aligned oracle card faceup in front of you. This is your anchor card, also known as your significator; it grounds the energy of your inquiry and focuses it squarely on the High Priestess. Pick up the rest of your deck and shuffle. While you shuffle, think of a question and bring it into your mind's eye. Some sample questions are:

- What knowledge that was once hidden is now open and available to me?
- Where should I focus my feelings about connection today?
- How can I hold sacred space for my growing light?
- Where can I find support and comfort in my day-to-day life?

Go ahead and pull a card for each of these questions, then line them up as if they were a four-card spread. Although each of these cards are an answer unto themselves, together they unlock the deeper message the ocean priestess has for you. If each card is just one part of the story, what is the complete message the ocean priestess is telling you? To sort this out, think about one or two keywords per card just to help narrow the meaning down. Write these keywords in your journal and use them to craft a sentence with the ocean priestess's message.

This wraps up your time with the ocean priestess. Make sure to take a small break before you dive into the next chapter. Allow yourself some integration time, as your energy has moved and shifted. You have done a lot of work, even if it doesn't feel like it, so be kind and gentle to yourself. When you are ready, the mermaids and I shall see you on the next page.

three
THE SEA WITCH

There is something very interesting about an edge: it looks suspiciously like a middle. Even if you look at your body and all its physical glory, the edge of your body is merely the middle between the physical matter of your flesh and whatever it will touch or interact with. So it is not surprising that in this chapter, you will notice similarities between edges and middles. The sea witch lives on the edge, yet they also live in the middle, for the sea is an edge and a middle. It makes sense that in this chapter we will also be discussing the first quarter moon; the edge of light touches the edge of darkness to create the middle, which binds them both.

Keepers of the edge (in this instance, the sea witch) are also the keepers of balance, harmony, and peace. It is the keeper's job to make sure that all those on both sides are happy, healthy, and well, meaning that the sea witch also needs to be deeply anchored to the present moment to access their intuition and incredible powers of foresight. That is why we will work through the third eye chakra in this chapter. Even though I consider myself a full-time fringe dweller—always experiencing life at the edges of possibility—everyone eventually finds themselves living, experiencing, and engaging with parts of their life from the edge.

Remember that there is an edge to what we know, to our lived experience. There is an edge and a limit to what we perceive and what is yet to be understood. If anything, *this* is the edge, the middle ground, the point of expansion that all humans and merfolk share. In fact, one could even argue that all sentient beings share this experience. Even the planet we live on has an edge to it, a space between what we know as our earth and what is unknown, which we call the Universe. The sea witch understands this, for they deal with both "what is" and "what could be" all the time.

The sea witch dances in the waves of calm and chaos, wild and tamed, safe and dangerous. This balancing act is not for show—it is real work that keepers of the edge take extremely seriously. There is a lot of responsibility that comes with keeping the balance and maintaining harmony and order. Only a select few can live in this space permanently, for the weight of this responsibility isn't something many wish to carry.

Even in everyday life, the edge is never far away. We are only one thought, one feeling, and one action away from the edge of what we know and what we do not yet understand. Lucky for us, the sea witch will be there with open arms to help us decide which side we wish to stand on.

Mermaid Archetype: Sea Witch

The sea witch is, in many respects, the elemental sister of the hedge witch. They are both fringe dwellers, boundary keepers, and protectors of wild spaces. The sea witch is the water to the hedge witch's earth. The hedge witch sits at the edge of a village and is the protector of the boundaries between unknown lands and domestic, organized settlements; she is the keeper of the earth's edges. The sea witch is her sea sister. This makes the sea witch profoundly important in the Mermaid Pantheon, for it is the sea witch who keeps borders and boundaries secure, stable, and moving. Travelers rely on the passage and protection the sea witch offers just as land dwellers rely on them to keep the shore free of trouble and turmoil. Because they are the go-between for the ocean of potential and the land of mundane existence, they had better understand their power, for there is no time for doubt in the sea witch's domain. Second-guessing can cost lives and abundant opportunities. To stand in the shoes of the sea witch means to stand strong, decisive, and unwavering in the face of discontent.

Just like their land sister, the sea witch has community tasks they are responsible for. These can range from birthing, healing, and mediating between different dwellers of the sea. It is not uncommon to find a sea witch surrounded by a healthy and abundant kelp forest, where life is bursting forth and water is at optimal oxygen levels. Sustainability and living in harmony with the seascape is the life path of the sea witch—what surrounds them will not only nourish them, but all those who come to their door. The sea witch's doorstep is a very busy place, as they tend to be the first to be called when members of the community have issues. It could be that someone is in need of a healing elixir or a word of advice, or perhaps it is time to bring new residents into the world while seeing other residents out of the world. Transitions are part and parcel of the sea witch's daily work because the sea witch understands the cycle of life, death, and regeneration. This is merely another edge the sea witch has to navigate.

It is not unheard of for the sea witch to be called when someone is in need of assistance, either to get back on their feet or start anew. Newcomers might first stop at the sea witch's door to ask for directions or advice, or to see how they can contribute to the larger community. The sea witch may live on the edge of activity, bumping up to the wilder parts of the sea, but this does not mean they are isolated, alone, or unaware. If anything, they know more about the comings and goings of their community than anyone else; it is how they keep the balance of the sea. This level of awareness comes from having a deep connection to the environment and to the merfolk around them. Although they don't need to be part of the daily drama, they are aware of the energy that moves and flows through the community they have sworn to serve. You see, the sea witch takes their role and their commitments seriously, so much so, they make it their life's mission to be of complete service to their community. This does not mean the sea witch doesn't have defined and enforced boundaries, because they do; it just means the sea witch sees commitment as an unshakable value they hold close to their heart.

There is no time for doubt and second-guessing in the sea. You are either committed to your course or you need to follow the tides and find your way. Or better yet, stay on shore until you can make a commitment one way or another. The sea is an unforgiving place, and one mistake could cost you your life. This is why there is no room for the sea witch to get distracted; there is so much at stake that they must give 100 percent day after day after day. Perhaps this is why there is only one sea witch per edge—this sort of work is only for a select few.

You need to be mindful when you walk into the sea witch's domain. You need to know why you are there and what your purpose is. And if you wish to step into their shoes for a while, well, then you need to make sure you are completely committed to everything that this archetype entails.

Devotional Practice

The sea witch takes their time so they can find clarity about their thoughts, feelings, and actions; it is how they maintain balance and flow in the ever-moving waters of the sea. They start their journey to clarity by asking questions, and not just any questions—*strategic* questions. Ones that are aimed to move them along the path from problem to solution, or uncertainty to certainty. Your devotional work with the sea witch will be the same.

Use the following journal prompts to start moving from where you are to where you wish to be. You can do this practice daily, once a week, or at the beginning and end of the month. Ask the sea witch for guidance and they will answer.

1. Where are the edges in my life?
2. How well am I navigating uncomfortable situations?
3. What tasks can I prioritize to keep me in balance?
4. Where can I delegate so I can stay in flow?
5. What pieces of my life am I keeping the shadows? Why?
6. How can I bring more of myself into the light and still feel safe?
7. What future vision do I need to hold to keep myself and my goals on track?

Set up your writing space however you want to; do what feels good for you as part of this devotional work. You might also consider lighting a candle and sitting near your altar while you journal, and perhaps having some tarot or oracle cards handy so you can pull one for each of the prompts. Cartomancy is such a large part of my devotional practice; I use cards for everything.

Moon Phases: First Quarter Moon

Balance is important, especially the balance between light and dark. The first quarter moon is a time to bring ourselves into balance, to settle into the new energy we have gathered from the new moon. It is the first opportunity we have had to plant both feet squarely on solid ground and draw the moon's energy into our daily lives. This settling energy is important, as it allows us to take a breath and take a look at where we now stand. This was much harder to do when most of the world was in darkness. But now, in the balanced light of the first quarter moon, the landscape is easier to navigate. That is why this is the moon phase of the sea witch: things are balanced, stable, and growing with light.

The sea witch can pull the lunar energy to the physical world and use it to illuminate what has been, what is, and the potential of what is to come. The future is still very much in the dark. For you see, in order to make magic, in order to do their work, the sea witch doesn't need to see the future. They only need to see where they are and what is possible from that position. That is more than enough for them to create ripple effects that will shape their future reality exactly the way they want it.

The first quarter moon is an incredibly powerful magical portal, and the sea witch knows this better than most. That is why they save their most potent rituals for this particular moon phase. Emerging light balanced with the darkness of rebirth is a time to reflect on what you are calling forth to be seen. What parts of yourself are you asking to step forward and be visible? Why is it important for this aspect of yourself to present, and how will it bring about a result or solution you are aiming to achieve?

These are all questions the sea witch asks before they even step up to their altar. First, they sit in quiet contemplation, making sure they are completely tapped in and tuned in to the energy they need and the energy they want to connect with. You, too, need to be this certain. Before you move into your ritual for this moon phase, take the time to answer the questions above. Journal about them, meditate on them, and allow the answers to be the grounding force you will need when you finally make it to your sea witch altar and enter your ritual space.

Ritual: Stepping into the Light

The magical items for this ritual may confuse you initially, but keep in mind that this is a stepping out ritual, which means there is physical action that needs to be taken in order to activate and maintain the magical energy, hence why this ritual calls for a pair of shoes. The shoes you select for this ritual will be the ones you wear and walk around in for at least a couple of days after the spell has been cast. These shoes will also represent the energy you are bringing into the light, so select your shoes carefully.

MAGICAL ITEMS

Two Candles: One black candle for the dark side of the moon and one white candle for the light side of the moon, as well as something to light them with

A Smoky Quartz Pocket Stone: This stone mixes and merges the dark and light energy

Pen and Paper: To write your incantation/mantra on

A Pair of Shoes: To walk around in

A Cup of Water: Any type of water will do

Peppermint Essential Oil: For motivation and movement

Place your shoes in the middle of your altar, with the black candle to the left of your shoes and the white candle to the right. (You may need to do this ritual on the floor if your altar is not big enough to hold your shoes.) Place your smoky quartz crystal on top of one shoe, or on the toe of the shoe, and set your cup of water at the heel or bottom of your shoes. Place three drops of peppermint oil into the cup of water.

On the piece of paper, write what part of yourself you are calling forth. Which version of yourself are you going to bring into the light? I highly suggest you write your answer as a mantra, affirmation, or intention statement. Here are some ideas:

- "With each step I take, I bring more of my confident self into the light."
- "I am a time walker, balancing my time with the power of the first quarter moon."
- "Every step I take brings harmony and balance to my life."

- "Magic is the step I take."
- "These shoes spread magic and light."

Write your mantra/affirmation/intention statement on the piece of paper, because you will be reciting it during the spell.

When you are ready to start your spell, light the black candle first, then the white. Repeat the following incantation:

I call on the power of the moon
The power of the dark
The power of the light
Balanced
Bring to me the piece of myself that
is ready to come into the light
I claim this version of who I am
I am ready to step into their shoes
With each step I take, I activate that version of myself
Growing in power
Growing in strength
Growing in light
With a balanced mind
With a balanced heart
I make this proclamation
[Speak your intention statement aloud]
As above
As below
The time is now
And so it is

Dip your fingers into the cup of water and peppermint oil and flick the spray over both shoes. Do this three times.

If it is safe to do so, leave everything where it is until your candles have burned all the way down. If you do not have a lot of time to wait for your candles, use birthday candles, as they burn super fast. Once your candles have burned down, you can put on your shoes.

Each time you put on your shoes, say your mantra/intention statement. Carry your smoky quartz in your pocket while wearing your shoes. Do this for two or three days. Document how it feels to be walking around in magical shoes. Notice if you feel, think, or act differently as you wear your magic. The sea witch is always documenting their work because this is how they refine, balance, and strengthen their magic. Now you will do the same.

Once your three days is up, you can put the shoes back in your closet. The magic will have worn off by then. If you want to deeply cleanse them, you can leave them outside in direct sunlight for a couple of hours or place them on a salt tile. It is entirely up to you.

Energetic Alignment: Third Eye Chakra

Here in the domain of the sea witch, it is time to go beyond what you think you know about the chakra known as the third eye. We are not using the third eye chakra for psychic voyeurism; instead we will tap into its more advanced technology. For too long, the power of the third eye has been taught at a very basic level. This energy center has the ability to change your entire life if you know how to access its power. The sea witch knows how to use this energy center to create worlds. They know it has the capability to bring things out of the vibrational plane and make them real. They also know that to awaken the advanced technology of this chakra, you need to understand which lower chakra is its companion. For you see, to really activate the magic that lies in the third eye, you must first come to understand that it does not work alone. It requires a key. A secondary power source. One of your lower chakras will unlock the true power of your third eye. The stronger that lower chakra, the more powerful your third eye will become.

But let's back up for a minute. The third eye chakra, in its most basic form, is the center of your vision. Not your regular vision, but the vision beyond the edge of what you can see with your physical eyes. This inner and second sight is what most people learn when they first start using this energy center. The inner vision allows you to tap into the lens of perception from your lower chakras, so you are more aware of the things you desire, crave, need, and want. The second sight also tends to show you glimpses of the worlds that live on the edges of our own, the worlds of spirit, light, and vibration. It is here in the second sight that people stay stuck. Although this sight can be helpful, it is limited in how it can truly assist you in your day-to-day life. This is why I tend to see the third eye chakra as psychic voyeurism. What I and the sea witch are interested in when it comes to this energy center are the third and fourth sight that are available to us. Your second sight is more like background noise; it's fun but distracting.

Your third vision goes beyond the noise. It is the vision beyond the vision. This sight or vision lets you move past the noise, past the distraction, into the energy of the soul. The sea witch spends most of their time looking through soul vision because it shows a world of possibilities, a world they can direct their currents toward. The sea witch charts a course in their sea so that all who sail in their waters will stay pointed toward their mission, their purpose, the reason they are here in physical form. Soul vision shows the bigger journey, with all the little karmic stops and starts along the way. Yet it does not dwell in the past, only showing the map of what is next and what could be. It offers multiple paths, multiple experiences, and multiple ways to get to the same place. Soul vision is like being able to see the branches of your very existence grow right in front of you: No doubts. No excuses. No baggage. Just infinite highways of pure creative potential.

For those who want to move even deeper, who are seekers of true enlightenment, then the sea witch offers a fourth sight: the sight of the awakened, where all is nothing and nothing is everything. Very few people gain fourth sight from the sea witch, as it is not really a sight. Nothing you will see at this level of the third eye will make sense; it will never be logical to you unless you have also upgraded your lower chakras to the point of being able to decode, hold, and maintain the new vision matrix. It is also not a sight you can use all the time, as you would never be able to do all of your mundane human tasks with it. Fourth sight screws with your physical sight and is actually seen with your eyes wide open. It is not a pleasant experience, and you sure don't want it to open up while you are driving.

For the sake of this book, the sea witch would like to invite you to expand your second sight and introduce you to your third sight. The sea witch would like to open your third eye energy up and refine it so you don't become overwhelmed by all the new experiences that will come your way. To do this, we need to revisit your lower chakras.

As I said at the beginning of this section, the trick to your third eye is in the energy center it is connected to. The lower chakras act as anchor points for the upper chakras. The stronger your lower chakras, the more powerful your upper ones become. This is one of the mistakes most people make when trying to open their third eye: they keep all their focus on the top chakras but don't bother with the lower ones. This, in turn, weakens the upper chakras and dulls their abilities. Your chakras do not work as islands.

The following exercise is a simple and quick way to find out which of your lower energy centers is the anchor point for your third eye. Once you know what it is, you will need to make sure it is as strong and stable as possible to leverage your third eye chakra's potential.

Healing Exercise

Although this is a quick meditation, you can definitely lengthen it and go deeper with the process once you have become more comfortable with opening up the third eye and holding the energy between the third eye and its connecting chakra. This meditation will help you understand that no chakra operates by itself. Your seven main chakras and the thousands of smaller energy centers throughout your electromagnetic field all work in conjunction with one another, which means that if you have one faulty chakra, or one center of energy that's blocked or not acting in the way it could, then there are gonna be problems in other areas of your electromagnetic system.

In this meditation, we are just going to focus on connecting your third eye with its lowest chakra companion. This will help you start exploring beyond what is called "psychic vision" to embrace your sea witch sight. Sea witch sight is everything that is beyond the edge of your psychic vision; it is deeper, more expansive. It gives you the ability to see beyond your limitations, beyond your ego perception, beyond what the conscious, unconscious, and subconscious can comprehend. There is an entire realm waiting for you to tap in, but it can only be done when you start to deepen, strengthen, and solidify the connection between the third eye and its lower chakra companion. With that said, let's begin.

Get comfortable. You can do this meditation lying down, sitting up, or in a comfortable yoga pose. Just make sure that whatever position you are in, you can move your arms freely. When you're ready, place your left hand just above your third eye, about an inch from the forehead. You don't actually want to be touching the skin; you just want to hold your hand close enough that you can feel the energy build under the third eye.

Gently close your physical eyes and block out the sensory information around you. Take three deep breaths, inhaling through the nose and exhaling through the mouth. Focus that breath through the third eye. Imagine air blowing through the chakra point in the middle of your forehead. Depending on how strong your imagination is, you might even be able to get some sort of sensory feeling in the palm of your hand. As you exhale, you might feel a little puff or wisp of air on your hand.

As you focus even deeper on your third eye, imagine indigo light starting to beam out of your third eye onto the palm of your hand, slowly and gently opening and expanding that third eye center. Now take your right hand and start scanning your body from the heart down. What you are feeling for are any shifts or changes in temperature around your body. You might also feel tingling sensations in your hand. When you find that change in temperature or tingling, stop scanning and place your hand in that area. Which lower chakra is that area connected to? If your hand is resting around the stomach area, it's going to be the third chakra, the solar plexus chakra. If your hand is around the pelvic area or the hips it's going to be the second chakra, the sacral chakra. If your hand is on your legs, that's actually the first chakra, the root chakra.

Keep your hand there, on that connecting point. Don't touch the skin; just hold your hand about an inch over where you felt that warmth, all that energy pulsing or shifting, and keep it there. Take three very deep breaths to the count of five.

In through the nose, one, two, three, four, five. Out through the mouth, one, two, three, four, five.

In through the nose, one, two, three, four, five. Out through the mouth, one, two, three, four, five.

In through the nose, one, two, three, four, five. Out through the mouth, one, two, three, four, five.

Steadying the breath, drop the hands. Roll out the shoulders and relax the jaw. When you are ready, you can open your eyes. The meditation is complete.

If you wish to take this meditation a step further, after you have connected the chakras, drop your hands and see if you can push the limits of your third eye vision. See if you can get glimpses beyond where it finishes—beyond the edge. Go beyond the vision. What you seek is beyond the ego vision; it is waiting for you on the other side. Now that you have connected your third eye chakra and activated your sea witch sight, you can start to see things that were once beyond your third eye's capabilities. Do this practice safely and gently—don't push your third eye's limits for longer than five minutes at a time as you build strength, stamina, and awareness.

Place of Power: Sea

You may very well be wondering what the difference is between a sea and the greater ocean. Like an ocean, the sea washes up to shore. It is traveled by boat and is often used for transportation and entertainment. It has depth and moods, but it is smaller. A sea is contained by more land than an ocean, which is why you will find a sea at the edge of the ocean. If you look at a map of the world, you can clearly find the various seas. You can see their containment points and where they eventually open up into the vastness of an adjoining ocean. This makes them fringe dwellers. Seas are an entity in their own right, but they're not connected to something so big they get lost or swept up. The sea is the perfect place to contain and maintain control over your magic. This makes the magic more potent and powerful. When something can be contained, it can be amplified. This allows the sea witch to turn up the intensity of their magic before releasing it into the vastness of the ocean.

This is a fabulous lesson for all magical uses, to be honest. Oftentimes, we get so caught up in the end result we are after that we forget the resolution we truly seek is inside us, contained in our own personal emotional and mental sea. When we stop and focus on this area only, we can create a bigger, more intense blast of magical energy.

At the beginning of this chapter, I likened the sea witch to the hedge witch. The hedge witch plays a very specific role in the community. The hedge witch does very specific magic and is a keeper of the edges. The sea witch is the same, and so is the sea in which they reside. The energy here is specific; so is its magic. That might be why it is confined to limited space. When you think about everything you have learned in this chapter, what sort of magic would you like to explore with the sea witch? Remember, it needs to be intentional, contained (at least for now), and related to what happens beyond what you know or feel is possible. Let's start by taking stock of where you currently are. The sea knows where it is and its boundaries.

Where are you? See if you can pinpoint exactly where on your journey you are. Think of using your third eye chakra to zoom in on your soul's location like a car's navigation system zooming in on coordinates. Once you have located your soul's journey, follow it until you can't see any more; that is your edge. That is where you start and where you finish. Now let's see what magical tools are available within that space, for this is your current sea, the space between. What moves freely through this space, and how can it help you create magic that goes beyond your edges? Let's dive deeper into this with your spellwork.

Spellwork

This spell is best done either at the beginning of the month or on a Sunday evening, so you can gather your magic and your magical tools for the week ahead. It really does depend on where in your schedule you would like to place this particular magic-gathering spell. Remember, we are talking about using what is at your disposal and what is available to you right now in order to create something that is not within your field of vision at the moment. We want to pull the unknown from the other side of the edge and bring it into your daily life. So make sure that you know if you're calling in magic for the week or magic for the month.

Gather some visual representations of your intention for the week or month, or take some notes. You need to know why you want to bring magic into your week or month. What purpose will it have, and how do you want it to assist you with your daily tasks?

You might start by writing out what the main projects you are working on and the parts you need to complete this week. I wouldn't put more than three to five big tasks on your list for the week because you want to make sure that you have enough time, space, mental clarity, and emotional energy to get these tasks done. If you are doing this spell for the coming month, then maybe you want to think about what big challenges are coming your way this month and how you want to break them up so they do not interrupt your productivity or flow for the month.

Next, gather visual representations of all the magical tools you are going to need to help you bring magical sparkles to your week or month. Maybe you're going to get up an hour early to get all these tasks done, or maybe you are going to go to bed an hour early so that you get enough sleep to power through your to-do list; you could choose a picture of an alarm clock as a visual representation. Perhaps you're gonna head to bed an hour earlier so that you can get some extra work done; you might choose a picture of a person in pajamas with their laptop. You might even consider gathering images of healthy foods or prepped meals so that is one less thing you need to think about. Whatever your magical tools are, you're going to bring everything into your personal sea and create magic, so collect a visual representation of everything you think you'll need.

Once you've gathered all your pictures, quotes, and whatever else you need, you can place them in your journal and create a spell crafting page, or you can put them on a small vision board. Cut and paste these items together. Play around with the layout.

Perhaps you want to doodle on the vision board or add stickers; get creative.

MAGICAL ITEMS

Your Vision Board or Journal: This is a visual representation of all the magical tools you'll need

An Indigo Candle and Something to Light It: This color activates the energy of your third eye chakra; if you can't find an indigo candle, white will do just fine, as white can stand in for any color

Your Phone or Laptop: Because we are gathering magical items and activating them to help bring magic into our lives, you might want to add your phone or laptop to your altar while you do this spell; I often add my iPad to my altar, as it is my main work device. Even our digital devices are vessels for magic and miracles

Once you've set your vision board or journal, your candle, and any other items on your altar, you are ready to begin your spell.

Take three deep, slow breaths in through the nose and out through the mouth while you place your right hand on your heart and your left hand over your third eye. These three slow breaths will connect your back to your body and the present moment as you project your vibrational body to the edge of what it knows.

Light your candle and recite the following spell:

Sea witch I call to me
That which is needed to set this intention free
Bring me tools from the other side of the edge

Send them my way
Fill my day with magic and miracles
From the land to the sea
From the ground to the sky
From the self to the void
From all the places the edges reside
Grant me this petition
Let me see
All that is complete
All that I need
So it is said
So it is done
My spell to the sea witch is now done

Ideally, you want to let your candle burn all the way down. If it is safe to do so, let the candle burn down before you remove any items from your altar. If you can't leave your candle to burn all the way down, wait eleven minutes at the very least before blowing it out. Then say something along the lines of "As I blow this candle out, my petition raises to the ears of the sea witch through the smoke, and so it is done." Then you can grab your phone or laptop off your altar and get back to work.

Leave your journal and vision board on your altar until the candle is burned out. Once your candle has burned down, pack up your altar. Keep track of any miracles that take place after you've cast your spell; document all magical items, situations, people, or opportunities that crossed your path. And thank the sea witch, for they not only heard you, they answered you.

Mermaid Connection Exercise: Journaling with the Sea Witch

The sea witch shows us how to make our wishes come true while being of service. There is magic in being of service to one's community. It's almost as if giving and receiving are linked somehow...

The sea witch may take their work seriously, but that doesn't mean they do not have a sense of humor! As you integrate the lessons of the sea witch, remember to do so with play and laughter. This is the edge the sea witch inhabits and how they maintain their boundaries. It is also where balance can be found within the first quarter moon. Now is a good time to reach for your journal and reflect on what you have learned about yourself while working with the sea witch.

- What does my heart truly wish for?
- Where can I be of service in my community?
- What will balance look like for me?
- What are my boundaries, and how am I maintaining them?
- How can I tap into more magic?

Think of these prompts as an act of service to yourself, opening up communication between you and the sea witch. Allow the answers to create space for more discussion around issues and topics like in-between spaces, manifestation, and what it means to be of service. There is magic in letting the words spill onto the page. Once you feel complete, move onto the cartomancy work.

Cartomancy: Nine of Cups

Nine of Cups

The sea witch has a magical quality to them. In many ways, they grant wishes, though not the ones we think we want—the ones we *need*. This aligns the sea witch to the Nine of Cups card in tarot. This is the card of asking for what you want and trusting the Universe will send you something even better. Being a cup card, there is a level of emotion, though it is contained and full of purpose. In other words, there is nothing random or haphazard about the results one gets when this card shows up in your life. If you are not a tarot person, you can use an oracle deck. Find a card that has to do with wishes to embody this energy.

Place the Nine of Cups card or an aligned oracle card faceup in front of you. This is your anchor card, also known as your significator; it grounds the energy of your inquiry and focuses it squarely on the Nine of Cups. Pick up the rest of your deck and shuffle. While you shuffle, think about one of your wishes. When you feel ready, draw three cards to create a spread.

- Card 1: The Nine of Cups or your aligned oracle card
- Card 2: Your wish in its current energy
- Card 3: The positive energy of your wish fulfilled
- Card 4: The unexpected energy of your wish fulfilled

Cards 3 and 4 have very important information in them. One will show you how to feed your wish, and the other will show what could show up that you may not have taken into consideration. You could even consider this the consequence card, as all wishes have consequences or a price to pay. This is not always a bad thing, but it is often unexpected.

If you feel like doing so, grab your journal and write about the cards you drew and the information they provide. Then, if your wish comes true, you can return to your journal to reflect on the spread's messages.

This wraps up your time with the sea witch. Make sure to move your body and get some fresh air before you dive into the next chapter. Your energy has moved and shifted. You have done a lot of work, even if it doesn't feel like it, so take a moment to breathe and connect to your body. When you are ready, the mermaids and I shall see you on the next page.

four
The Siren

There are times in our lives where we find we do not speak up for ourselves. We do not ask for what we want, or we swallow our opinions because we don't want to make waves. Then there are times when we can't seem to stop the word vomit from happening. We have all experienced these moments; they are part and parcel of navigating this crazy journey we call life. As technology advances and communication changes, humans are finding themselves navigating multiple new ways to communicate with one another. Sometimes this is a blessing and increases efficiency and clarity in our exchanges with others. Then there are the cases when new ways of communication make things more difficult—if you have ever had to navigate one of those customer service bots, you know what I mean. Language, speech, and how we listen and hear are changing rapidly. Yet, despite it all, one thing has not changed: the role the throat chakra plays in our ability to communicate not just with others, but with ourselves. A master of the throat chakra is the siren.

The siren calls to us in our waking and sleeping time: whispering in the wind, singing in the rain, chirping with the birds, and dancing with the moon. The siren is the sound itself. The frequency of vibrational energy is audible. If you think about it, the siren invented sound healing therapy—it was just misunderstood by those unaware of its purpose and intent. I guess we have technology to thank for our deeper appreciation of the siren's song. Now we know how different pitches and frequencies resonate throughout our physical body. We have a deeper awareness of how sound can heal, transform, and reprogram our minds, and how it can change the way we feel and heal. Sound healing is so mainstream these days that musicians have started to imprint siren frequencies into the body, mind, and soul; tantra and hip hop come together in the song "You Me (444 Hz)" by Maejor and White Sun, for example.

In this chapter, you will learn how the siren is already doing their healing work in your life, and how you can intentionally call the siren to assist with communication, consent, and manifestation. We will also work closely with the waxing gibbous moon, connect with the throat chakra, and learn the magic of the waterfall. As the planet becomes more and more polarized, we could all use the assistance of the siren to listen, learn, speak, love, and transform into more open and compassionate beings.

Mermaid Archetype: Siren

Not all sirens are the same. When I was researching sirens, I kept finding conflicting accounts of what a siren was and what mythological lineage they belonged to. Each country had slight variations in their stories, and each ancient story seemed to tell the tale of the siren in slightly different ways. After days of research, I came to the conclusion that there is more than one type of siren. Some do not fall within the parameters of the Mermaid Pantheon, but one or two absolutely do. Maybe those within the merworld should be called singers, not sirens, for their songs do not lure—they heal. They do not cause chaos; they calm. These sirens of the mermaid world are not interested in destruction. Instead, they are service-based merfolk who only want to heal, restore, and bring some form of light into the world.

The sirens of the Mermaid Pantheon are creators and healers. They are a gift to those under the waves and those who are fortunate enough to receive their song on land. No two songs the siren sings are the same. Each song is unique, for it is the healing song for the being or entity that has called to them. If you know how to connect with the siren, they will share your healing song with you, teach you how to sing it, and upgrade the healing power inside your own throat chakra.

Perhaps this is why so much siren mythology speaks of luring people to the edge of danger, as you need to see what is causing you pain in order to let it go. Myths, folklore, and ancient storytelling often use metaphors to speak about the human experience. People wrote songs, ballads, riddles, and chants that cautioned those on the edge of some sort of breakthrough. Oftentimes, these warnings hinted at the right path to take—the path that would stop you from crashing or landing in even more danger. The siren has the same mission.

I like to think of the siren or mermaid singer as one of your guides, nudging you toward the right path. The siren sends you music to follow so you can navigate out of harm and into healing. I can get lost imagining the siren's voice calling me out of a mental fog and into the clear waters of inspiration. The siren is a beacon of hope when nothing around you is clear and your eyes are struggling to see. They ask us to see with our ears and navigate with our voice. The siren is not the only underwater being to do this; whales and dolphins use sonar or echolocation to navigate, chart migration paths, and find lost loved ones. Perhaps there is even more to learn from the siren than we first thought.

Devotional Practice

In this chapter, we will explore the growing light with the waxing gibbous. Another way of looking at light in relation to the siren is that they are guiding you to the light, showing you a clear and unobstructed path out of the darkness. In this respect, you could say the devotional path of the siren is to raise your voice and allow it to be heard out in the open, where everyone can appreciate it.

This can be likened to waking up in the morning. The more we become awake, the more light we slowly let into our lives. The more conscious we become as we move into waking, the more we become aware of the thoughts, the inner narrative that is circulating in our mind. Each morning as you awaken, you affirm what sort of day you will have. You either affirm your busyness, your stress, or your lack of energy to tend to all the demands the light brings, or you can start your day with a siren song, one that sets the tone, energy, and mood for your day. Your siren song can be an actual song, a mantra, or a musical meditation. Listen to it the moment you start to hear the inner chatter beginning.

This might sound like a far-fetched devotional practice, but I assure you it works brilliantly. In 2020 I participated in a morning chanting circle. Our group would meet online at 4:30 every morning and start our day with two mantras, both set to beautiful music. It was the most powerful and profound practice I have ever done. I honestly believe it is why I ended up with so many creative projects and financial opportunities in 2021, most of which will carry on for at least the next three to five years. That is an incredible return on my three-month investment! I do not doubt for one second that I was riding the frequency current of the siren. And now it is your turn.

Choose your siren song wisely. Make sure the lyrics, tones, and melodies are creating the impact you wish to create. If you'd like, you can sit in the same place each morning, light a candle, call in your siren guide, and listen to your song. If it is not going to disturb those in your house or your neighbors, sing your siren song out loud. If not, whispering or singing at a very low volume will be just fine; I pretty much whispered my way through my three months of chanting, so I know you don't have to belt out a song for its magic to work. But hey, if you can raise your voice and open that throat chakra all the way up, I encourage you to do so.

Once your siren song is over, carry on with your day. If you keep a journal, I recommend recording your start date and the date you decide you want to finish this devotional work. Then document all that happens during that time. You might be surprised by what you find. If you do not journal, at the very least, mark on a calendar when you started doing this practice and when you decided to stop. You don't need to do it for ninety days like I did, but I would do it for as long as you can stick with it. And no, it doesn't matter if you miss a day here and there. I think during my three-month morning chant circle, I missed four or five days, and everything was totally fine.

The main purpose of the siren song is to change your inner narrative, to alter self-talk, to reprogram how you walk into the light of the day. The way I see it, you have nothing to lose and everything to gain by starting your day with your very own siren song.

Moon Phases: Waxing Gibbous

At this phase of the moon, it is pretty hard to hide its fullness and growing form. It is too large to hide in the shadows; everyone can point up to it and see it growing. If you think about your own life right now, there are probably areas that echo this waxing gibbous energy: areas where you have grown significantly and others can't help but notice. This is the moon phase that signals that your time for hiding is over. I talk about this particular moon phase as the time to open your mouth and yell your offer from the rooftops. For the sake of this book, you could say this particular moon phase is about opening your mouth and singing the song of your new creation. It is time to find the song of your life and to channel your inner siren so you can share it with the world.

The waxing gibbous is an active moon phase. By this I mean that you have to take some form of action. You may even find the energy during this moon cycle pushes you along, almost forcing you to keep moving, which makes this a great time to reengage with projects you have put to the side or to connect with people you haven't seen in a while. What could be more siren-like than picking up the phone and calling someone to come play with you? The siren wants you to get vocal, to share, to speak, to invite, and to alert the world of what you are growing and expanding in your life. Think of it as a creation celebration. Reveal your accomplishments to others and ask them to join you in celebrating. This sort of energy will only bring you positive vibes as you get closer and closer to the full moon.

Now is not the time to be shy, so slip on your best outfit, do your hair, clean your face, and get the camera ready. Limber up your body and, most importantly, practice your speech. Know what to say, when to say it, and who to say it to, for this is going to be vital under this particular moon phase's influence. Not only are you connecting with your siren energy and the vibration of the sirens in the Mermaid Pantheon, but you are going to channel that energy. Let it flow through you and into your throat chakra. Let that energy infuse your vocal cords so when you open your mouth, you will be truly bewitching to all who hear you.

Ritual: Be Seen, Be Heard, and Release the Siren Within

This is a very simple ritual. It takes five minutes or less to do this ritual once you have your magical tools all set up.

MAGICAL ITEMS

A Blue Candle and Something to Light It: For the throat chakra and communication; white will do if you cannot find blue

A String or Ribbon: This will be tied as part of the ritual, so make sure you can easily untie the material by pulling it; color is not important here, as the knot is symbolic

A Glass of Water: You will be drinking this water, so make sure it is clean and, preferably, filtered

A Spoon: You'll need this to stir your water

Pick up your string or ribbon. As you tie a bow, think about the last time you found yourself in a situation where you did not speak up for yourself, felt powerless to use your voice, or just decided to stay silent on a topic and have regretted it ever since. Perhaps you are thinking about someone you want to apologize to but haven't, maybe because you don't know how or because so much time has passed you feel uncomfortable or awkward about it. The bow will represent this contracted energy around the throat chakra, an energy you are going to liberate under this moon phase.

Once your bow is tied and you have placed your energy into it, go ahead and get your glass of water and your spoon. Bring your bow, glass of water, and spoon over to where you are going to light your candle.

Take a few deep breaths and steady yourself as you imagine sending loving oxygen into your throat. Feel the breath as it hits the back of the throat, and feel it as you exhale the breath out through the mouth. The deeper the breath and the more oxygen you can move through that energy center, the more receptive your throat chakra will be to the words you are about to speak. After your third breath, light your candle and recite the following:

Siren of the sea, hear me
Siren of the sea, assist me
Siren of the sea, I call to thee
I am ready to release that which is stuck
I am letting go of what's in this knot
I'm opening my throat
I am starting my song
Siren, please heal me

As this knot is pulled apart
My true voice is now ready to sing
Siren of the sea
I give you this energy
Free me
As it is spoken
So it will be
My knot is no more
It is now done

Untie your knot and lay the ribbon or rope on your altar, or wherever you are standing or sitting. Pick up your spoon and start to stir your water. As you do, say a few potent affirmations and visualize the words floating into the glass and being stirred into the water. Here are some examples of affirmations you could use:

- I speak clearly and kindly.
- I am allowed to speak when I deem it appropriate.
- My voice matters.
- I use my voice as a tool for compassion and clarity.

You only need one or two affirmation statements; don't go overboard.

Once you are done reciting your affirmations, set the spoon down and drink your water. You can drink it all in one go or space it out over the course of the day. There is no wrong or right way. I like to down my water right after I infuse it, but do what feels right for you. Your ritual is now complete.

Energetic Alignment: Throat Chakra

Throughout mermaid mythology, sirens, which were considered masters of illusion, lured sailors to their own personal wreckage. The lesson in these myths isn't that sirens are dangerous, but that what you allow to seduce you may lead you down a path you never recover from.

Your ears are connected to your throat chakra; what you hear effects what you say or don't say. What you allow yourself to listen to will influence the stories you tell, the beliefs you form, and what actions you take, which is why your throat chakra is where your center of consent lives. Consent is what you allow, agree to, listen to, and say yes or no to. There are some pretty heavy energies that surround the throat chakra, and the siren is here to help you navigate them without ending up wrecked on the rocks of your life.

First, take an audit of what you are listening to. It is easy to let our consent boundaries slip when it comes to our ears, but it is important that you really pay attention to the constant noise in your life. We are bombarded with noise in the modern world, from TV to radio to social media. Someone somewhere is wanting your attention and trying to influence what you consent to. This is why leaving the TV on while you sleep is the worst thing you could possibly do. This noise is programming your brain; it is setting up neurological pathways of belief in your mind and, without you even noticing it, it is refining what you say and how you speak about issues in your life. If you must listen to something while you sleep, take a page out of the siren's song book and find a healing mantra, chant, or piece of music that is set to healing, positive, and life-affirming frequencies.

Sound is so powerful that it affects all our cells. I had the honor of working with one of the pioneers of sound therapy for years before she passed away. I saw firsthand how certain frequencies affect our cells, how sound can turn on and off certain codes that can make cells well or sick. When you are sleeping, your mental and energetic bodies are wide open and receptive to any and all sound that is floating around, so do your future self a favor and raise your awareness around this issue. Be intentional with what you allow in your bedroom while you slumber.

The next thing you need to look at is what you are reading. Now don't get me wrong, I love a good fiction book just like the next person. Sarah. J. Maas, Susan Dennard, and V. E. Schwab are real-life literary goddesses in my eyes. But I'm not really talking about fiction, as we know consciously that it is made up. When it comes to nonfiction, I am very intentional about what I read and condition my brain with. I am very careful how much news I consume and how much endless scrolling on social media I indulge in. The latter is probably the most seducing, to be honest. If we wanted a modern-day siren fable, look no further than the endless social media scroll, or the addiction to validation by checking how many people liked a post. This sort of behavior is ripe for wreckage. It disempowers the energy in the throat chakra and trains it to not speak unless it is rewarded. For women and minorities, this is damaging in so many ways, as it sets up a code of consent that says "I cannot speak unless someone likes what I have to say." Which, in turn, means these groups are less likely to speak up when they need to. Prejudice strips away one's ability to communicate openly and clearly. When we don't all have the same right to speech, the world becomes a very one-sided place.

Your next siren audit is to monitor how you speak, when you speak, and what words you use inside your head. Yes, this audit is for your outside *and* inside voice. For the most part, people's inside voice is the most toxic. How we speak to ourselves is very rarely, if ever, monitored. If you tear yourself apart every time something goes wrong, before you know it your internal siren song is one of self-loathing, and crashing headfirst on the ragged rocks becomes inevitable. There aren't many times I recommend being Pollyanna about things, but when we speak to ourselves, it sure wouldn't hurt. Imagine blocking out all the negative self-talk, letting go of all the anger and resentment you have for yourself, and instead talk to yourself like you are the most special snowflake in the Universe.

You may not be aware of this, but what you watch, what you read, and what you allow in your ears sets the baseline for how you speak to yourself. The good news: it's easy to change. The bad news: it's not simple to maintain. This level of siren awareness needs to be intentional, deliberate, and done every single day until you have developed a whole new set of healthy throat chakra habits.

Everything we have talked about in this section is a habit. These are habits you have more than likely been unaware of. You have probably not given these sorts of behaviors too much thought, as you didn't truly understand the complexity of the energy you were absorbing. If, however, you were already pretty aware of all this, trust me—there is always room for improvement. Even I catch myself sometimes. Especially with the social media stuff; it really is so easy to get lost down a scrolling rabbit hole. So don't think this is a "one and done" choice; it is a new level of life.

Modifying these habits might be challenging at first, but it will get easier as you start truly tapping into your inner siren. You want to be creating deliberately. You want to speak from a place of compassion and purpose. And most of all, you want to be the master of your own life song. You will set those notes and consent to the frequency, and when you are ready, you will turn the volume up and blast it into every cell of your body.

Healing Exercise

Before you bemoan the whole affirmations part of this process, let's discuss it. I know there are going to be people reading this book who honestly believe affirmations are a complete and utter waste of time. I get it. I do. Just bear with me. What if I was to tell you part of me agrees with you? Affirmations, in their purest form, the words, do very little at all. The magical part of the affirmation process is the emotional charge created by your belief in the words that come out of your mouth. This is how affirmations end up becoming what you believe and not the words you speak.

Let's break this down ever more and use a simple three-step process. This is a process that can be done anytime you think about your intentions or goals, or even when you set abundance and money goals for the month. The process is very simple. It goes something like this: we believe what we want is possible for other people, we believe what we want is possible for us, and finally, we believe what we want is inevitable for us. If we aren't somewhere between the "possible for us" and "inevitable" stages, affirmations are a complete waste of time. The truth is, unless we're in that space, we just don't believe what we are saying. Disbelief then programs the throat chakra to reject all future words of want around this subject.

You may not like to hear this, but your beliefs are habitual. You aren't even conscious of them most of the time, but your energy body remembers and sets up the automatic response based on your most intense emotional charge. This is more problematic for complex affirmations, which we will not get into in this section. Instead, we are going to focus on leveraging your habitual beliefs and expanding them inch by inch toward your inevitable goal. You have to get both your conscious and subconscious to say yes to something, which is why for this exercise you are going to focus on single-word triggers or generic affirmation statements. Keep in mind that the siren is more interested in expanding your belief in your words than anything else. The mermaid singer wants you to believe everything you say. They want you to receive a resounding *yes* throughout your conscious and vibrational being. And to do this, we start small.

This siren throat chakra healing takes about seven days to ease into, though I would highly suggest you work with it for at least thirty-three days. You are going to want to think about your time in a 40/60 split. For the first 40 percent of your time, you are going to focus on one word only. The remaining 60 percent of your time will be focused on a generic affirmation. Over the course of seven days, that means the first three days would focus on single-word affirmations and four days would focus on generic affirmations. Over the course of thirty-three days, that amounts to fourteen days of single-word affirmations and then nineteen days of generic affirmations.

Right, now that the math is out of the way, let's talk single-word affirmations. As I write this book, I am currently in the middle of the thirty-three day version of this technique, and my single word has been *change*. You see, I am working on stopping myself from clenching my jaw. Every time I notice myself tightening up my jaw, I yell the word *change* inside my head and instantly stop.

So, first things first, what do you want? You gotta be honest about this. For me, it was that I wanted to be free from physical pain. Pull out some paper and write down what you want. Just write one thing. Pick whatever has the biggest emotional charge to it—you need to really care about it.

Now that you've written what you want, pick your word. It should be based on the action you need to take. I picked the word *change* as word because my action is to change my response. I am emotionally linked to this change, so *change* is my emotionally charged word. Your word could be anything.

Right now, I am about ten days into this process, and I have noticed some very interesting side effects of repeating the word *change* multiple times a day. My mind has started to process differently—in other words, changing how it would normally problem-solve or think—allowing my daily life to change along with it. I am sure this would have been the same if I had selected the word *adapt*, *transform*, *transmute*, or even *grow*. So far, it has been a really positive and fascinating thing to watch unfold.

Once you have done your 40 percent of days with a single-word affirmation, it is time to move into doing the simple and generic affirmation. For those of you who do work with affirmations, I know you are going to be skeptical of the term *generic*. You might be yelling at this page "But it has to be specific!" Again, we are looking at healing and reprogramming your inner siren. We need to move the thing you want into the "it is possible *and* inevitable for me" columns. To do that, super-specific, complex affirmations will be hit and miss, whereas generic affirmations will build your belief muscle and amplify the "yes" magic in your throat chakra. Let me give you an example of a couple of generic affirmations I use when I am researching an idea for a book or deck.

1. "I seek out things that inspire me today."
2. "I will have inspiring conversations with those I interact with today."
3. "I am attracting something that will spark and ignite me today."

As you can see, these are very generic. None of them speak about writing, ideas, or trying to prove something right or wrong. There is no problem-solving and no way these affirmations can fail: I can always find something inspiring in my day, I can always have inspiring conversations, and it's very easy to attract something, anything, that might spark me—I mean, a piece of cake will do it! I'm not a complicated person. Yet all of these affirmations are emotionally charged;I really want to be inspired. When I use these, they always work. This book is proof they work.

Now it's your turn. Write your generic affirmation. Think about using words like *attract*, *will have*, *seek out*, *observe*, or even *listen for*. These are action words, and they are important to add to your siren song. Words create movement, so give them a direction and a purpose.

Don't try to be too cocky with this. Stick to one or two affirmations. Don't go overboard and create ten or twenty. You don't need them, and the more you create, the less chance you have of growing the belief muscle. Repetition is the key here. That is what sets the current program in your throat and that is what will reprogram it. Keep it simple. The siren knows true magic happens in the simplest of things.

You are now equipped with your healing words. Go forth and sing, whisper, yell, or simply talk your way to a new siren experience. Just don't forget to mark your calendar when you start, and look for evidence of things shifting as you progress.

Place of Power: Waterfall

Since I moved to the United States from Australia, I have become somewhat of a waterfall hunter in the early spring months. A waterfall, by definition, is when a body of water or ice melt drops vertically over a slope or multiple slopes. This means waterfalls, unlike other bodies of water, are not contained to the same rules as lakes, rivers, or even oceans. Some of the most beautiful waterfalls I have seen are smack in the middle of the desert. In early spring I can see a waterfall just twelve minutes from my front door here in Las Vegas, Nevada. That, to me, is what makes waterfalls the most magical bodies of water on the planet, and it's one of the reasons I have linked them to the power of the siren here in this book. Waterfalls bring magic to the most unsuspecting of places. Now don't get me wrong, I totally appreciate waterfalls no matter where they are. But there is just something incredibly magical about finding them inland, in unexpected pockets. I have visited beautiful inland waterfalls in Utah, Oregon, upstate New York, Colorado, and North Carolina. "Inland waterfall chaser" might be my new lifetime quest, to be honest.

There is a certain amount of drama to a waterfall, especially when it is in full flow. The water sings—sometimes even roars—as it crashes over rocks and falls through tree leaves. Then there is the rhythmic way it splashes to the ground or into an awaiting pond. Of course, the height, depth, and type of waterfall will play a part in the song it sings. Waterfalls take time to form. Unless they were created by a flood or an earthquake, a waterfall generally takes quite a bit of time to create itself. Erosion plays a vital part in this process, as it wears down the water's path and forms the perfect conditions for the waterfall to sing.

Just like the siren, a waterfall in full flow can stop you in your tracks and make you pay attention to what is in front of you. The drama, the noise, and the spray all have the ability to grab your focus and keep it. This is the waterfall magic we are going to focus on for our spellwork: the ability to stand in your power and let your song flow, and allowing others to stop and soak it all up.

Spellwork

This spell is a seasonal one, meaning this spell should be done under the first waxing gibbous moon of spring. In many ways, this spell is to set the tone for your coming year, starting with the emerging seasonal light and the melting of the snow after the winter months. This is when the world starts to flow again, when all those who have been huddled indoors emerge and rejoice in the new life budding all around them. What better time to dust off your vocal cords and sing your very own song? The good thing about doing a spell once a year is you have plenty of time to prepare the lyrics of your song.

Part one of this spell involves opening your mouth and speaking, singing, or asking for what you want. Part two is about allowing others to hear you, being attentive to what your words are saying, and offering others space to respond. This is a bit of a big deal, which is why you are taking your cue from the waterfall. It flows because it has worked hard for the space to do so. The waterfall knows it has earned its moment. When you open your mouth, you have earned your time as well. All you are doing is claiming your time, space, and moment.

MAGICAL ITEMS

A Blue Candle: Use blue for the throat chakra; if you can only find white, that's perfectly fine

Fresh Flowers: Wildflowers or flowers from your garden will do just fine

A Vase: Make sure the vase is large enough to hold your fresh flowers

A Watering Can: Fill this with water to represent the waterfall

Pen and Paper: To write your song lyrics

The first step is to write your song lyrics. Your lyrics should explore all the thoughts, feelings, and experiences you are laying down for the year ahead. You want to make your lyrics count, so break up the verses for different parts of your life. For example:

- Start your song by calling forth the power, love, and magic of the siren.
- Verse one could be about family or relationships.
- Verse two could be about health or well-being.
- Verse three could be about money, finances, or career.
- Verse four could be about vacation, play, or experiences.

- End your song by giving thanks to the siren and release your spell to the mermaids.

Your song's chorus needs to be your mantra for the year, and you want to repeat it after your verses.

Now, if you are thinking you don't have what it takes to write your own song, you can do this another way. Find a song you love and print the lyrics. Edit, switch, and adjust the words so they embody your own year ahead and then use that. This is for your own personal use—you won't be sharing it—so you will be fine doing it this way, if that is what you choose. I'd encourage you to give writing your own song a go first, though.

Once you have your song written, you will need a light blue candle for the throat chakra. You will also need a bunch of fresh flowers and greenery and a vase to put them in; don't put the water in yet, because we will be doing that as part of the spell. If fresh flowers are really hard to find, use a houseplant that is healthy and needs to be watered. Finally, you'll need a watering can with water in it; this is going to be your waterfall. Here we are mixing the elements of new growth, new life, flowing water, and your voice. This is a powerful combination, so prepare yourself for some potent magic!

You can do this spell at your kitchen table or outside; make sure you're somewhere you have room to lay out your flowers and where using water won't be a problem. To start and activate your spell, light your candle. Then start singing your song while you arrange your flowers in the vase. Pour water slowly into the vase, creating a waterfall effect from your watering can. Complete your song and set your vase wherever you'd like it.

If you are using a houseplant, water it very slowly while you sing and then return it to its normal spot in the house. It will love being infused with your song and magic—houseplants adore being part of rituals and spellwork.

If possible, leave the candle burning. If you feel guided to, move it to your altar. If you don't have a lot of time to wait for your candle to burn down, consider using a birthday candle, as they burn very quickly.

Now that your spell is complete, you can go about your life. Keep your song lyrics somewhere safe so you can check in once a year and track how your spell is doing. You only need to do this once a year; your song set in motion everything that needed to happen to make your lyrics come true. It's okay if not everything in your song comes to pass in the first year. Be patient. Trust the siren and know that the path is open.

Mermaid Connection Exercise: Journaling with the Siren

There has been much work done during this chapter. You have explored how, when, where, and why you use your voice; what sort of things you give consent to; and perhaps you've even tapped into your very own siren healing song. This feels like a good time to crack open your journal and reflect on what you have learned about yourself while working with the siren.

- What are you speaking into your life, and how is it emerging?
- Where do you feel scared, limited, or restricted in asking for what you want?
- How do you deal with rejection?

- How can you embrace the energy and flow of the waterfall in your daily life?
- When do you find yourself speaking your power?

Think of these prompts as ways to start the reflecting process. Do not feel limited by these questions; allow your answers to open up more discussion. Let your thoughts flow freely. There is magic in letting the words spill onto the page. Once you feel complete, move on to the cartomancy work.

Cartomancy: The Moon

The Moon

The energy of the siren is deeply connected to the Moon card in tarot, which has the energy of dreams, cycles, and things that go bump in the night. If you are not a tarot person, you can use an oracle deck that aligns to the energy of the Moon for the following spread.

Place the Moon card or an aligned oracle card faceup in front of you. This is your anchor card, also known as your significator; it grounds the energy of your inquiry and focuses it squarely on the Moon. Pick up the rest of your deck and shuffle. While you shuffle, think about how you use your voice and what you would like to create with it. When you're ready, pull two cards.

- Card 1: The crossing. Place this card on top of the Moon card so that the cards make a cross-like shape. What is crossing the energy of your throat? This card shows you what energy is currently dictating the terms of your siren song.
- Card 2: Place under the cross. This card shows you how you can clear this crossed/blocked energy, if it is energy you do not like, or how to leverage this energy, if it is positive and agreeable to continue using it in your life.

This simple spread gives you a very quick snapshot of the energy around your throat chakra and helps you find your siren song. If you feel like card two didn't you enough information, you can draw one more card and ask for additional guidance. Do not draw any more cards than that, as this is meant to be a quick check-in.

This wraps up your time with the siren. The mermaids and I recommend taking a small break before you dive into the next chapter to allow yourself some integration time. You have done a lot of work, even if it doesn't feel like it, so be kind and gentle to yourself. When you are ready, the mermaids and I shall see you on the next page.

five
The Common Mermaid

There's something about having an open heart that requires such a high level of vulnerability, a feeling of being exposed in a way that would make most of us feel uncomfortable. Yet being able to measure our level of receptivity to our level of vulnerability is incredibly powerful. Not to mention it takes an incredibly high level of courage to maintain this openness. When you move through the contents of this chapter, you might see how you live wide open, or it might bring to mind people who live wide open, people who have nothing to hide and bare it all for the world to see.

We all know people who are highly emotional, highly intellectual, or type A personalities. These people tend to go through the world as if they're running out of time. "Go big or go home" is their mantra. These people have no fear of laying themselves bare for the entire world to see, even if it's messy. They have what we call in this chapter *the mermaid heart*. It might've been broken, it might have cracks, it may even still be in the process of healing.

Yet despite its beating, the heart stays open and receptive, just like the shoreline. The shoreline, like the mermaid heart, stays open and exposed to the elements. Yet, somehow, it still seems to be full of magic and mystery, allowing itself to be the place where miracles can take place.

This chapter is in the middle of this book, just like the heart chakra is in the middle of the chakra system. And just like the heart chakra, this chapter stands between two worlds: the world of what you have read and the world of what you have not. The heart chakra mediates between the world of the lower chakras and the world of the upper chakras; it also bumps up against the borders of what is physical and what is vibrational: what is known and considered solid, trusted, and true.

As you move through this chapter, you may be challenged to think about concepts a little differently. The mermaids may ask you to keep your mind open, and your lens of perception may need to be adjusted slightly. But most of all, you're going to be asked to tap in, tune in, and turn on your mermaid emotions, for it is time to go deep. It is time to dive! It is time to explore parts of who you are and who you could be at the edge of who you think you have become. Limits will be tested, boundaries will dissolve, and you may discover things about yourself that you didn't know before. The mermaids are playful, so their form of discovery is not meant to be hard or harsh. Here in the realm of the common mermaid, there are no falsehoods or truths. In this space, everything is possible; every point of view, every opinion, can be given equal space and equal weight. There is freedom here if you want it.

Your decisions while in the realm of the common mermaid will affect the direction of your life. You see, the mermaid heart and the shoreline are not places that you can dwell. They are places you visit, places you come to pay your respects, or even places you explore—but then you leave. You don't live in the middle of the story; you move either toward the future or back into the past. The mermaids will always encourage you to move toward the future, to push toward what you do not yet know and to be brave and receptive to all that is possible—even if it is beyond your point of knowing, beyond the edges of your existence, and beyond the next beat of your heart.

Mermaid Archetype: Common Mermaid

I know using the term *common* when talking about a mythical creature like a mermaid seems a little strange. I mean, how can a mermaid be common? Within the Mermaid Pantheon, though, the mermaid is known as common, as they are the bulk of the population. As we all well know, when something is everywhere and easy to find, it is considered common. Humans are pretty common; we are everywhere and pretty easy to find. However, just because something is common, it does not mean it is not special. Just because there is a lot of something doesn't mean it has no value. And just because it is easy to find doesn't mean it is not precious. In many respects, this is what the common mermaid is here to teach us: within our common existence we have value, we are special, and we are precious. This could end up being the most important gift of all from the Mermaid Pantheon. Despite everything, you are prized, loved, and needed, despite the fact that there are over seven billion other common humans on the planet. Needless to say, there are some serious heart lessons to learn here, especially when it comes to finding one's place in the crowd.

One of the things I found very interesting while researching the common mermaid was the debate over how humans represent the mermaid, and by that I do mean physically. There are many who believe that the tail is all wrong, that the more humanoid features could not exist without gills, and that we may even misunderstand the physical nature of the mermaid. It got me thinking about how we don't even really understand our *own* physical nature. There is so much about a human we don't know, and it seems the more we learn, the more questions we have. Just like mermaids, the physical nature of humans is hotly debated. The common human is a varied creature, much like the common mermaid. People aren't really that similar if you were to start breaking us down, yet we all seem similar because of the way we organize, live, and engage with life. So could it be that mermaids are exactly the same? Maybe there are those that fulfill the scientific way they are thought of and those that don't, but perhaps they all kinda blur together because of the way we see them?

This leads us to the main point of this entire chapter: to truly understand the common mermaid and even the common human, we need to move from the mind and drop into the heart, for the understanding we seek is deep within our heart center. The heart is very common. All living beings seem to have them. In fact, they are as common as rice, bread, and dirt. Yet you cannot exist without your heart. Your body needs it to keep functioning. So even though your heart is common, it is magical. Are you starting to see a theme here? Common things may be the most magical of all, be it the common mermaid, the common human, or the common heart that beats inside your common flesh-and-bone chest. So perhaps it is fitting we have a very common devotional practice for this section.

Devotional Practice

This is the prayer to the common mermaid. It's a sacred script that speaks about the ordinary, everyday, little things that are easily overlooked. To do this prayer, you can just recite the script. Or, if you want to be a bit more fancy, you can light a white candle and then recite the script. The whole point of this prayer (and this entire chapter) is to keep it simple and easy. Focus more on the intention, not the act.

I am stopped
Movement paused
My head drops
Humbled by the miracles
Ordinary things making magic
Hand on heart
Breath of life
All that has become manifest
What lives
What grows
What loves
What dreams
Is blessed in this moment
A common day
A common life
A phenomenal existence
And so it is

Moon Phases: Full Moon

The spotlight has arrived and all can be seen with perfect clarity. There is nowhere to hide under a full moon. The light is bright, open, and shining on your every move. This shouldn't bother you, though, because you have been working your way through the Mermaid Pantheon and know that now it is time to stand in your full mermaid form and show off all you have created, worked on, or accomplished. It is your time to shine, mermaid, so do not be shy about it! The world has been watching you grow, waiting anxiously for your big reveal, and now it's here. The best part of this moon is you really don't have to do much of anything. Just stand under its light and let it illuminate you.

Mermaids are playful and curious by nature, and that is the perfect way to approach all of this new light shining on your life. Let your inner child out and explore all that is being revealed right now. Be curious. Wander. Don't worry about anything that isn't currently in the light, for this is not the time to explore the shadows. Just like you won't be able to hide under the bright light of the full moon, neither will anyone else. Before we had street lights, the full moon was the biggest social event of the month. Dinner parties, events, and celebrations were held during this moon phase because it clearly showed the safe path of connection. For mermaids, this is still true. All things you wish to connect with have a safe path to them, and if you can open your heart to them, your feet will guide you toward them without any real action from you.

Granted, not everyone likes to be this exposed, and for some of you, this bright world may not seem to be your friend. That is why it is even more important for you to come back to that playful space, to allow yourself to play with the light, and to create a space of celebration.

If being out in the world just isn't your thing, throw a party for one or an intimate dinner party with friends. However you decide to play in the space of the full moon is entirely up to you—

just make sure you do. Don't allow this powerful moon phase to slip on by without leveraging it for your mermaid success. To prepare for your full moon playtime, do the following ritual and let the party begin!

Ritual: Full Moon Party for One

Growth needs to be celebrated. Now that the spotlight is finally on you, it is time to take a moment and soak up all you have achieved. Learn to initiate celebration in your life rather than waiting around for others to do it for you. Mermaids know this, which is why they are always up for a party, even if it is a guest list of one. You see, the mermaids understand the notion that the more you celebrate all the good that is happening in your life, the more of it you get to create and, in turn, celebrate all over again! You doesn't always have to celebrate big, huge, massive success; you could (and should) celebrate small, mundane, everyday wins that fill your heart with joy and a sense of purpose. The more your heart is filled with these higher octane feelings, the happier and freer you will feel.

MAGICAL ITEMS

Pen and Paper: To write down happy moments from the last few weeks; you may want to do this in your journal

A Candle: Use a pink candle, if you can find one

For this full moon party of one, start making a list of everything you have done since the new moon that filled your heart with joy. Write down all the actions, thoughts, connections, and conversations you have had over the last couple of weeks that made you feel good to be alive. They will have moved you into a feeling of purpose.

I am always surprised by the events that make me feel this way, because they are never the ones I logically would have thought. Sometimes it is spending time attending to my plants, giving them a trim and watering them. Other times it is sitting on the floor surrounded by books and coming across the perfect quote or message for the day. Other times it is a morning laugh with my wife over breakfast, or a silly text from a farm friend about their chickens and ongoing hen drama. All of these things fill my heart with joy. They all make me feel connected to life, which is a cause for celebration.

Give the full moon permission to shine its big, beautiful light on these moments. See them. Feel them. Bask in their emotive energy. These are the moments that push your heart wide open.

After you've written your joyful moments down, celebrate them. One of the best ways to do this is to light a pink candle, which is for celebrating joy, and to read your list of moments out loud. Say something along these lines:

Full moon, thank you for shining a light on
All the ways my life lights up my heart
I see clearly people, places, and things I wish to celebrate
From the turning of the new moon
I celebrate [the items on your list]
In celebrating these moments of my growth,
I am connecting back to the flow
of my mermaid path and purpose
I give thanks to the water goddess
And all those within the Mermaid Pantheon
And so it is

If it is safe, you can leave your candle burning. If you do not have time to wait for a candle to burn down, consider using a birthday candle. If neither of these are an option, you may blow the candle out and consider your ritual complete.

Getting into the habit of celebrating under the full moon mermaid-style will only add to the magic in your life. There truly are no downsides to adding a party of one ritual to your monthly routine.

Energetic Alignment: Heart Chakra

The heart is the middle connection point in your chakra system. It is what connects the upper and lower chakras and is the center of communication between the high realms of thought and consciousness and the lower frequencies of the ego and material world. In many respects, the heart keeps the balance and does its best to be the peacekeeper of your entire electromagnetic body. Your heart works really hard, even when you are asleep. Your heart is the first spark of energy that ignites in your physical experience, and it is the last light to blink out as you leave your body and go back to vibrational form. Your heart carries all your joy and all your pain. It is both bright and light and cracked and weighty. There is no doubt it is the toughest part of all living beings.

The heart of the mermaid, which is not the same as the human heart, is a special thing indeed. In this chapter we are going to explore the lessons the mermaid heart teaches that we can adapt to our own human heart. The mermaid heart is naturally open, even during difficult times. The mermaid heart is self-repairing and honors all cracks, breaks, and tears. It infuses these imperfections with the mother of pearl and creates a radiant beating, living gem.

The mermaid heart understands that diving deep into connection leaves one open to pain, yet they continue to do it anyway. Mermaids love connecting with others. They thrive on adding people to their social circles and expanding their heart-centered community. Community is family to the mermaids, and they know in order for their species to thrive, they need to focus on more than just basic biology. Heart energy is so important to the merfolk that they work tirelessly to make sure everyone in their community is taken care of. Having an open heart means having an open mind, but this does not mean that there are no boundaries, rules, laws, and regulations. In order for a true heart-based community to thrive, there has to be rules, order, and limits, but it is how these are done that make the difference. The mermaid heart is not naive; it knows not every single person will be happy 24/7. The mermaid heart understands that for some, their path is not heart-aligned, but even this difference is taken into account, and pathways to connection are always left open.

The mermaid heart may be able to break, but it will never shut a door. It will never close itself off and shut down. There is true strength in keeping your heart open even when you don't really want to. This is the power of love. Love for yourself. For when you let love in, no matter how painful, you will never be left alone. Prolonged isolation can be harmful, and the merfolk know this, which is why they focus on community. Even the most reclusive curmudgeon needs someone to check on them once in a while! When one sees that their life has value, then they see life as an asset. This causes a chain reaction inside a community, one that is life affirming. In turn, the community becomes more attracted to things that make them feel alive. This extends into the environment they live in, for when one is connected to self, they also become connected to place. Place is where life happens, and when you want to enjoy life, you become protective of your place. Keeping an open heart has incredible rippling benefits.

What comes naturally to the mermaids may not come naturally to you. It may not seem normal to you to keep your heart open. It might feel uncomfortable to shift your focus from you and yours to those you don't know. You might be resistant to thinking about your role in the condition of the world around you. That is okay. That is why you have this book and this connection to the mermaids. The mermaids are here to help, to assist you in repairing, healing, and resetting the energy of your heart. They are also here to give you an open invitation to join their community. They know that the very act of buying this book was a desire to belong to something larger than yourself, even if you don't think you can open your heart wide just yet.

The more I connect with the mermaids, the more I learn more about the importance of community, of what it means to belong and matter. They teach me how to be strong even when things seem hard. They show me the support that surrounds me even when I feel like I have to do it all by myself. They are a constant beat in my heart, and knowing that they are there has changed how I see my heart energy.

Just like some of you, my heart has been broken. Sometimes those breaks were caused by other people. Sometimes they were caused by me. I understand more than anyone what it is like to feel the need to close down your heart and leave it closed forever. I know what it is like to feel like I had to place locks, walls, and barriers around my heart in the name of protection—and I know how wrong I was in that thinking.

When my life fell apart and I closed myself off to the world, I got sick. Very sick. So sick that my body started to turn on itself. I was prodded, poked, and tested for months on end, only to have medical professionals draw a big fat blank as to why my body was shutting down with no real indication that it could be stopped. My human heart was broken. It needed to repair. I believe I was being influenced by the mermaids even then; they placed people and situations in my path to help me heal. I'd like to tell you healing was a bed of roses filled with unicorns and rainbows, but I won't lie to you. I am still repairing my heart. I am still moving through moments of deep and profound sadness around my past. The path to recovery was not, and is not, an easy one. But the return on investment is worth it.

Now the mermaids and I offer this gift to you. The path is right here; we have paved it with light so you can't lose it. All you have to do now is walk the path one small step at a time, whenever you are ready.

Healing Exercise

A broken heart is a common heart. We all have breaks in our heart energy; we have all been let down, hurt, and even wounded. To walk this mortal plane means accepting a broken heart as a common experience. Just because a broken heart seems to be a common human experience, it doesn't mean your pain is common, nor does it diminish your suffering. It does, however, remind you that you are not alone. Everyone who walks beside you is beating with a cracked heart. As you move into healing this part of you, know that you will help your community heal as well, for the mermaid heart beats through your community. The light and energy of the mermaid heart will flow into you and through you as it opens your heart, tending to its many breaks, cracks, and fractures.

The best part of this healing energy is that it can be done anywhere, anytime. All you have to do is hold your hands over your heart, close your eyes, focus your breath through the heart center, and imagine the mermaids sending healing light right into your heart. Hold this small meditative healing for a couple of breaths and then move on. Do this whenever you feel yourself closing off or when you need to feel connection with mermaid energy.

One of the happy offshoots of doing this heart healing is you may very well connect with and join your mermaid healing guide, so pay attention to who might drop into your imagination as you do this practice. If you see the same mermaid or group of mermaids, know that these are your healing mer-guides. If you don't see the same faces each time, then the merfolk are letting you feel love from a wide number of community members.

Place of Power: Shoreline

The shoreline is a magical place. It is the place where two worlds meet, where the land finishes and the water begins. Yet this is a bit of an illusion, for the land does not end, it dips. The water does not necessarily begin, but some would say the shore is where it ends. There is a merging, a leaping, a spiraling of beginnings and endings all coming to the same point on the shore.

The shore is where humans stand and cast their gaze out to the sea and wonder what happens below the waves. The water is where the mermaids lift their heads, gaze at the land, and wonder what it is like to walk around on two legs, to be rid of their tails and scales for a while. It is the shoreline where we dream, where we give thanks, where we rest and restore. There are even plants, birds, and wildlife that live only at the shoreline. It is a specific ecosystem all its own—a world within worlds. Present, past, and current moment. The mundane, miracles, and mystery all find themselves on the shoreline. It is almost as if time itself merges here, allowing anyone who stands at the shore to be anchored into the moment yet drift to both the past and the future.

Maybe this is why so many people are drawn to the shoreline. We can get lost in the rhythmic lapping of waves. Perhaps this is why time seems to disappear while we play along the shore. I will admit I lose hours sitting on the sand. Time has both stood still and sped up all while I just sank my toes in the sand and allowed myself to be cleansed by the spray of the ocean. My wife and I seem to be constantly called back to the shoreline, even though we live in the desert. We hear the call in our heart and are always compelled to respond and present ourselves to this magical in-between space.

For those of us who have mermaid magic running through our veins, the shoreline is the portal to a world we are always trying to get back to. Maybe that is why it calls us so. No matter what I do or where I roam, I will always end back at the shoreline, gazing into the waves and watching and waiting. When I needed inspiration for my *Animal Totem Tarot*, I walked the shorelines of northern California. When I was working on the *Mermaid Tarot*, I spent hours wandering the shoreline of southern California. In my twenties when I needed to heal, escape, and feel whole, I found myself at the shoreline of the southern Victorian coast. There is no doubt that when I need to feel one with my soul, the shoreline calls.

The shoreline is a busy place. It is filled with a lot of foot traffic, not just of humans but birds, wildlife, and the occasional sea creature. From sun up to sun down, the shore is one of the busiest places to be. There is a constant amount of movement and energy in the shore as the tides wash in and sweep back out. What is interesting about the sorts of activities that happen on the shoreline is that they are all very intentional. Be it walking, wave gazing, sunning, feeding, or collecting stones and shells, everyone seems to have an intentional purpose, albeit common and mundane in nature. I guess you could say the shoreline is where common, everyday magic happens.

Spellwork

For very practical reasons, you do not need to be at the shoreline to do this spell. Instead, you are going to create your own shoreline. Magic is symbolic, so we don't need to be at the shoreline to enjoy its benefits; really all we need are the elements that make the shoreline.

MAGICAL ITEMS

A Small Jar: I recommend a glass jar with a lid

Sand: To represent the beach—this must be sand; do not substitute

A Bowl: To represent the ocean

Water: Any water will do as long as it is clean

Items that Remind You of the Shoreline: Suggestions include stones, shells, or even a photo of the shoreline. If you do not have these items, that's okay; they will not make your spell any less potent

A Green or Pink Candle: This connects your spell to your heart chakra; consider getting a birthday candle if you won't have time to leave it burning

Pen and Paper: To write your intention statement

We discussed earlier that when people come to the shoreline, it feels intentional. Many feel like there is a clear purpose for being there, even if it is just to feel the sand between their toes and the sun on their face. You too will need an intention for being at your magical shoreline. It could be to bring more peace into your life; it might be to remind you to move and exercise your body; it might be to slow down and reconnect to the joy in your life. Whatever it is, write down your intention. Just know it should be a simple intention, one that is connected to your day-to-day life. There is no space at the shoreline for complex things. This is a place for tangible, mundane, common things, so make sure your intention matches that.

Now that you have all your items, including your intention, put water into your bowl. It should not be overly deep; add just enough to cover the bottom. Next, place your jar in the bowl. Add sand, your intention, and any other items to your jar. When your jar has everything in it, put the lid on and close it.

Secure your candle to the lid of your jar. This is done by lighting the bottom of the candle and allowing the wax to melt and drip onto the lid, then holding the candle in place till the wax cools. If you have a small candleholder and feel safer using that, place the candle in it and set it on top of your jar.

Take a moment to settle yourself and prepare for your spell, breathing in through the nose and out through the mouth as you drop your shoulders and relax your jaw. Imagine the sound of the waves hitting the sand. Conjure the sounds and smells of the shoreline in your mind. Immerse yourself in this sensory visualization.

Open your eyes and light your candle. Recite the following:

At the shoreline I stand
Drawing its power to me
Wind in my hair
Sea at my feet
Arms wide I give my heart to the
Mermaid, oh mermaid come to me
In this moment
Set me free
This space in between
The want and the need
Here on the shoreline
I can just be
Mermaid, hear my heart
Feel my intention
Prepare me to move
To the beat of the mundane
In motion to the magic
That flows from the sea
Everyday thoughts fill my mind
Simple yet magical
As life will be
Let these words free
So it is said
Mermaids, so it shall be

To end this spell, stand in silence with your hand on your heart for a few more breaths, then gently roll out your shoulders.

Allow your candle to burn all the way down if it is safe to do so, and get on with your day.

Mermaid Connection Exercise: Journaling with the Common Mermaid

There has been a very heartfelt chapter. You have explored your human heart and seen what lesson the mermaid heart has to offer. You have celebrated under the full moon, visited the shoreline, and felt the power of temporary healing spaces. This feels like a good time to crack open your journal and reflect on what you have learned about yourself and your human heart while working with the common mermaid.

- Where do you want to bring more vulnerability into your life?
- How will you celebrate more in your daily life?
- How can you use the lessons of the mermaid heart to start your own heart healing?
- Where do you need to find more balance in your life?
- Can you identify where the middle ground is in your relationships with others?

Think of these prompts as a way to open up the dialogue with your heart center. Allow the answers to open up more discussion. Let your thoughts flow freely. There is magic in letting the words spill onto the page. This journal exercise may be one of the things your heart needs in order to start feeling safe. Once you feel complete, move on to the cartomancy work.

Cartomancy

Four of Pentacles

At the very beginning of this chapter, I talked about how the heart is a midway point in the electromagnetic field. It sits smack in the middle of your seven major chakras, and it is the communication point between the Universe/source/divine and the ego/physical/material. This spread is a quick and easy way to check in and see what messages your heart is channeling for you.

The tarot card I am using to anchor this spread is the Four of Pentacles. In many respects, this is the tipping point of the central nervous system. If you feel too vulnerable, this card will become you holding on too tight, like your heart is contracting. If you feel good about where you are, then this card can represent feeling safe and secure in your daily life, like your heart being open and willing to receive. If you want to anchor this spread with an oracle card, I would choose something that represents safety or vulnerability.

Place the Four of Pentacles card or an aligned oracle card faceup in front of you. This is your anchor card, also known as your significator; it grounds the energy of your inquiry and focuses it squarely on the Four of Pentacles. Pick up the rest of your deck and give it a shuffle. Draw one card and place it above the anchor card. Draw another card and place it below the anchor card. Then draw one last card and cross it over your anchor card.

- Card 1 (above the anchor): A message from the higher realms
- Card 2 (below the anchor): A message from the physical realm
- Card 3 (crossing the anchor): The message your heart is broadcasting to your central nervous system

Take your time going over your cards. You might need to open up your journal again and take some notes. Remember to write down how these cards make you feel. This is the heart we're talking about, after all, so it is all about feeling. I also recommend doing the common mermaid prayer after your reading.

This wraps up your time with the common mermaid. The mermaids and I recommend taking a small break before you dive into the next chapter to allow yourself some integration time. You have done a lot of work, even if it doesn't feel like it, so be kind and gentle with yourself. When you are ready, the mermaids and I shall see you on the next page.

six

The Shapeshifter

You are not the infant you came into the world as; you aren't even the child you shapeshifted into after infancy—you are a totally different person living in a very different world to the one you entered. Human shapeshifting tends to happen slower than the sort we think about when we think of magical shapeshifters; fantasy books and movies have made us biased when judging our ability to shift, change, transform, or even transmute. As humans, we tend to see our changes as inevitable. But isn't that the point of shapeshifting? It is inevitable to change forms. One of the things you will learn in this chapter is that shapeshifting is cyclic. Every form has its time and reason, but it doesn't necessarily coincide with the timing you feel is appropriate.

Time is such a weird and wobbly thing in the realm of the shapeshifter. Nothing in this part of the Mermaid Pantheon is going to follow a linear format. This means the archetype of the shapeshifter might challenge those of you who like order, structure, and organization. And the energy of the solar plexus chakra burns through this chapter, only amplifying this nonlinear energy, which is often out of our control. So hold on tight, as you are in for a bit of a wild ride in this chapter, and some of you might want to duck into those ever-growing shadows brought about by the waning gibbous moon.

I am going to ask you to do your best to sit with any and all discomfort that bubbles up while working with the fiery shapeshifter energy in this chapter. Remember when you had to adjust to that awkward stage of adolescence when you were not a child anymore, but you were not an adult either? During that time in your life, you had to navigate a constantly changing (and sometimes reactive) environment as you came to terms with who you were and how you fit into the world. Some of us made it through that stage of our lives better than others, but we did make it—it was just uncomfortable, a little alien, and very messy. Think of this chapter a bit like that. I'm not saying you will go through another adolescence—that would be a horrifying prospect—but stick with your emotions, the way they flow and move you in ways you didn't logically expect. Eventually you'll make it to the cooldown phase, when the cooling lava leaves something strong and stable in its explosive wake.

Finding new, solid ground is really the reason we go through change in the first place. So step up and enter the realm of the shapeshifter. Let them guide you to a new understanding of who you are and what you are capable of.

Mermaid Archetype: Shapeshifter

Shapeshifting and mermaid mythology go hand in hand. There are many tales of merfolk coming onto land and taking human form: tails turning into legs, scales turning into skin, and gills turning into breathing through the nose and mouth. This shapeshifting ability gives birth to the idea that merfolk can and do have the capacity to live in two very different worlds—an idea that most humans romanticize. I know I think about how cool it would be to move through worlds, able to seamlessly blend in and have different experiences at will. But the truth is, humans already do this. We probably do it several times a day. We just don't call it shapeshifting.

For the most part myths, legends and fairy tales have taught us to believe that shapeshifting is something physical in nature and that it might even hurt. Most people aren't passionate about pain, so I can see why as a collective species, we may be shy when it comes to our own shapeshifting abilities. Yet, people still romanticize the mermaid and their ability to move through worlds. But honestly, apart from the whole legs and breathing thing, the mermaid shapeshifter looks pretty much the same; if Hollywood has taught us anything, it is that they don't change much from the waist up! This means that even if you look and sound the same, you can still be a shapeshifter, regardless of what world you find yourself in. Which brings me back to my point: humans are natural-born shapeshifters, and this archetype is more aligned to our everyday experience than any other.

As you dive deeper into the energy of this archetype, I want you to think about all the different ways you show up and engage in the world. Think about the versions of yourself that you cycle through on a regular basis: partner, coworker, business owner, relative, parent, friend, and all the other hats you wear. In reality, each of these aspects of yourself shifts, flows, and transforms into someone specific. The you that presents for your children is not the same you who appears to your partner; you shapeshift from caregiver to lover and back again, inhabiting different worlds every time you shift.

Now, you might think this form of shapeshifting isn't anywhere near as impressive as being able to turn your legs into a tail, but the mermaids and I beg to differ. The shapeshifter wants you to really lean into the idea that you have an incredible superpower. You are able to transform and adapt to whatever environment you find yourself in, which is exactly what the shapeshifter does. This mermaid archetype offers you the space to truly explore the many versions of who you are, and you'll even explore the parts that you have been resisting. This archetype does have emerging shadows; there may be things you don't feel ready to show the rest of the world yet, but this might be blocking your shapeshifting abilities. You will have some time to explore that further in the waning gibbous section of this chapter. For now, just acknowledge that you may be carrying some fear around. This nod to the fear will be more than enough for you to move forward and start your devotional practice.

Devotional Practice

To start your devotional practice, you first have to admit to yourself that you are a shapeshifter. You need to allow yourself to lean into this reality so that the mermaids can mold your belief ever so slightly about what is possible for you.

Then, select a version of yourself you want to embody more often. Think of the you that doesn't get to be seen as much as some of the other versions of you. Let me give you an example. I want to embody the fun, fluid, and playful part of who I am, the me that feels good, joyful, and comfortable in my body. I don't allow myself to shapeshift into this version of me very often, but I'd like to. You can pick any version of yourself you want; it might be a seductive, sensual goddess or a confident money magnet. Just make sure to choose a version of yourself you do not show to the world very often because you feel some sort of fear, shame, or unworthiness.

Once you know which version of yourself you wish to embody more, pick up your journal and start writing down all the reasons this is so important to you. Really dig deep with this one. You have to know your "why" in order to follow through with any course of action. Take as much time as you want with this stage.

When you are done journaling, make a vision board for this version of you. It doesn't have to be very big; I recommend six inches by eight inches, or paper size A5 for all you non-American peeps. As you look through images to put on your vision board, think about how this version of you dresses, stands, eats, plays, works, feels, and wants to be seen. Get bold with this. Then glue your images onto your vision board.

Make sure you let your board dry before you place it where you want it. Perhaps you want it in your line of vision at your desk, in your bathroom, next to your bed, or even in your wardrobe. Where you place this vision board only needs to make sense to you.

The act of making space for this version of yourself is a devotional act. You do not need to do anything else. However, if you want to, by all means add a meditation, a chant, affirmations, or a crystal to the mix. You could even prepare an altar for this version of you and light an orange or white candle each day while saying an affirmation. Just know it is not necessary. Through the journal work and the creation of the vision board, you have completed your devotional work to honor the shapeshifter in you and in the Mermaid Pantheon.

Moon Phases: Waning Gibbous

Now that the energy of the full moon has left your sphere, it is time to take a breath. Exhale for a while and release all of the tension from your body. It does not matter whether you had a successful moon month or not; your body will have held on to some stress. So let go, exhale, and allow yourself to slowly uncoil from all the energy you have been pushing since the new moon.

Under this moon phase, you are changing, shifting gears, and turning inward instead of focusing outward. From this point on, all that you do will have a different feel, look, and energy to it. No more hustle; no need to put yourself out there; no building tension. Drop your shoulders and breathe.

Allow the other you—the busy, goal-oriented, results-focused you—to melt away. Replace it with a version of yourself that allows more space into your daily life. Slowly let the pressure of the last few weeks ease from your body. Shift your thoughts, thinking only about creating space. The waning gibbous is an indicator that the moon is not as full as it was. Just as the moon now shapeshifts, so will you.

The shapeshifter is about changing form, oftentimes physically, but they are not limited to this. Shapeshifting can be about the mind, the energy, and the emotion you have been traveling with. The moon is past the halfway point in its journey, and so are you. Right now, you may need to take time to see where you currently stand. So, let's do a quick check in.

How are you? Are you where you had planned to be? If so, how does it feel to be here? If you're not where you had planned to be, what happened? How did your journey veer off course? Pick up your journal and spend some time with these questions. Remember not to pass judgment on yourself as you write out your responses. Just hold space for the answers.

There is nothing worse than not allowing yourself to enjoy all that you have accomplished. Do not diminish your progress by focusing on what you did not complete. It is easy to focus on what is not there; the shapeshifter asks you to stay present with what is. Hold your ground and create space for all the blessings, support, and love that surround you, as this is the energy that shapes you. Focus on what adds value to your life. What gives you strength and fills you up so you can continue to grow? Keep in mind that there are no wrong or right answers to any of these questions. They are merely a way to gauge where you are, where you have been, and what needs to happen to make sure the next part of your journey motivates and inspires you.

I always think about this moon as if it is sweeping things off my schedule. As the light of the moon fades, so do my tasks. It is a very calming and peaceful way to think about the waning gibbous. Instead of the monstrous to-do list that normally greets me from the new moon to the full moon, now I have less and less to do. I have space to reconnect with my creative energy. I feel myself shapeshifting from chaotic to calm. My shoulders drop, my jaw unclenches, and I sleep soundly. It is nice to know that this particular moon phase indicates a time to wind down. Now it's your turn to let the energy of this moon phase sweep over you. Relax, release, and restore.

Ritual: Making Space

Once a month I do a massive desk and office clearing. I put away books I have been using for research, remove the sticky notes plastered all over my desk that are no longer relevant, sort print outs, and review my writing calendar and business schedule. I also use this time to clean my devotional spaces. This is my waning gibbous ritual, and now I am sharing it with you.

Even though it is not technically the end of the lunar month, there is something about opening up space after the full moon. In coaching, we call this "zooming out" so you can see what you have done and what is left. Oftentimes we are so close to our daily lives we don't even notice the clutter that surrounds us. But this clutter blocks opportunities, money, joy, and even people.

Performing a waning gibbous ritual each month will give you the space you need to breathe, and it will allow room for new and exciting things to come in before the lunar month ends. This act of cleaning, clearing, and pruning will also allow you to gently shift from the version of yourself who was all work and no play as you built momentum for the full moon. As the shadows start to grow, remove all things that could block the receding light. So get to it! Roll up your sleeves. It is time for you to create space and opportunity in your life by clearing away what is done and complete so that it no longer drains your energy.

Energetic Alignment: Solar Plexus Chakra

Your center of action is also your center of reaction, and I am sure I do not need to remind you that we live in a reactionary world. Out of all the chakras, it is easiest to know if the solar plexus chakra is out of whack. Humans with a healthy solar plexus chakra tend to have a pretty good grip on their anger; they are hard to trip up and tend not to overreact when things don't go their way. Those with an imbalanced solar plexus chakra are just looking for reasons to blow shit up. Think of your solar plexus chakra as your bratty self *and* your empowered self. As the ultimate shapeshifter, your solar plexus chakra will either make your life easier, or it will amp up your level of personal suffering. The good news is, most of what happens in this energy center is governed by the chakras under it.

It is normal to get angry, and I truly do believe there is a lot of healing energy that burns within anger. Life force energy is ramped up when we get angry. It floods into our physical vessel like a raging inferno. It is powerful energy that, if harnessed the correct way, can be incredibly creative. Unfortunately, most people have not learned how to use that energy to repair and restore.

This energy center is also where your courage comes from. When you think about it, that logically makes sense, as it takes tremendous courage to stop, pause, and reflect before acting. It is a true act of bravery to not respond when provoked. There is a higher level of consciousness that runs through the third chakra, and it is activated when one allows themselves to be courageous enough to be vulnerable. Now, don't confuse what I am saying here with allowing people to take advantage of you or walk all over your feelings—what I am saying is that when we take a step back and truly observe energy interactions, we can intentionally act from a place of self-love.

Everything that is triggered in the solar plexus chakra has consequences. There are no exceptions to this rule. You could even call it the energy center that creates your karma. You see, most people don't think too much about how they act. They are set to autopilot, for all humans are creatures of habit. Some habits are bad, some are downright destructive, some are neutral, and some are life-affirming. A good shapeshifter chooses their habits carefully, even the destructive ones. They are tapped into how they move through the world. They understand at a fundamental level that every action has an equal reaction—and a karmic consequence.

Nothing is done at an unconscious level for the shapeshifting merfolk. When you come and sit at the tail of the shapeshifter, they will expect you to be just as aware. Just as vulnerable. Just as courageous. They will expect you to know you are living an intentional life where *you* decide which version of yourself you will be at any given time. You must be tuned in to your actions and accept all consequences willingly. You can't hide from the shapeshifter. It doesn't matter what version of yourself you change into; they will still see all of you. They are your mirror.

This might be the easiest off-kilter chakra to notice, but it is not the easiest chakra to connect to on a deliberate level, because this is where you meet you. All of you. The devil and the angel. The version of you that is trying to be good and do better clashes with the version of you that is mad as hell, still reeling from past wounds and ready to burn it all to the ground. To say this is a volatile chakra might be an understatement. That is why the shapeshifter is here to help: to stabilize your fire. They know how to turn all that energy into something productive; they are masters at creating life where there was once destruction, which brings us back to vulnerability. In order for the shapeshifter to truly be of assistance, you are going to have to open up. Drop the excuses. Shed the coat of the victim and step into your naked power. Well, not physically naked, though you can do that as well if it is your thing. I am talking about being *soul* naked, without the ego trying to cover up all the little cracks, faults, and ugly parts of yourself.

So, are you ready? Can you step onto this level of the Mermaid Pantheon with your eyes wide open and you soul bared for all to see?

It is okay if you aren't ready yet. It is a lot to take in—we get it. You might still have work to do on your lower chakras. You may very well have to circle back to this stage. Just know this: the seed has been planted. Your awareness has been cracked open. And even though you may not be ready today, you will be soon.

To help, the shapeshifter has some healing work for you. Think of it as prep work, work that you can do now even if you aren't ready to go deeper. The following healing exercise is the first step on the path to making a deeper connection with your solar plexus chakra. It is where you begin, but it will not be where you end.

Healing Exercise

Now that you are more aware of how the shapeshifting energy works in the solar plexus chakra, let's think about how you want to show up in the world. This healing exercise asks you to lean into both your triggers and your solutions. Remember, everything you do (or do not do) here in the third chakra has consequences. So, as your emotional triggers show up, your shapeshifter mer-guide would like you to practice burning them away to reveal the solution hiding inside.

For this exercise, you will need a journal and a pen, or if you are more digitally inclined, your iPad and a stylus. It is important you write and not type, as it is more healing to let the energy move through your hands and into the pen, pencil, or stylus.

On the morning of the day you'd like to do this exercise, start a list. As you go about your day, write down all the ways you find your solar plexus chakra reacting during the day. These could be situations that make you angry. Perhaps someone disrespects you, annoys you, or creates feelings of low self-esteem. You will also need to be on the lookout for any time you become defensive or feel paralyzed and unable to act. All you are going to do during the day is collect these situations and the feelings that arose from them.

In the evening, come to your altar or mediation space and sit with your list. Have your journal or iPad nearby. Write down the phrase "I will not judge myself for" and add one of that day's reactions to the end of the sentence. (For example, "I will not judge myself for getting angry when so-and-so raised their voice at me.") Do this for all of the reactions on your list. When you have written all of your responses for the day down, take a moment to see if anything else bubbles up. If so, let it out in the pages of your journal.

When you feel like you have run out of words, put your pen down and take a couple of deep belly breaths. Allow yourself to relax. Place your hands over your belly. Close your eyes and visualize the situations that caused the reactions you just listed. You do not need to focus on all the things you listed; perhaps there is one that holds more reactionary energy than the rest. That is the one you might wish to focus on for this session. Do what feels right in the moment. Remember, you are not judging your responses or reactions—you are leaning into them so you can create a healing response to your triggers.

Once you've chosen which reaction to focus on, call the shapeshifter mermaid to you. Ask them to assist you by burning this reaction away to reveal the blessings. This might happen while you are doing the exercise, or the blessing will be revealed over the course of the next few days. Normally it doesn't take long.

This exercise doesn't need to be long. Two to five minutes is more than enough. If you want to stay longer in this healing energy, by all means do. Once the exercise feels complete, shake out your hands. Thank the shapeshifter for their assistance, roll out your shoulders, and breathe normally.

You might consider doing this every waning gibbous as part of your lunar practice. It is good to create space within you just as it is to create space outside of you. Of course, you do not have to wait for a waning gibbous to do this healing. You can do this exercise to reset and restore your solar plexus chakra or whenever you feel yourself becoming overwhelmed with emotional triggers. Trust your inner shapeshifter to know when to do this exercise and for how long.

Place of Power: Lava

It is easy to forget that right under your feet is a bubbling world, a liquid world flowing with fire and destruction—one that is so aggressive it can wipe all living things off the planet. This under-the-crust ocean is called magma, and when it bursts through the surface we know it as lava. Now, we are not going to get into the science of lava in this book. Instead, I am interested in the shapeshifting abilities of lava. There are many shapeshifting components of our earth, yet none of them are quite as dramatic as lava.

This burning-hot liquid has the potential to create new worlds and ecosystems, and it can even shapeshift the landmass around it.

Lava is a builder, sculptor, and abstract artist. Lava starts off as a burning liquid, flowing as a river that destroys everything in its path. Eventually, it cools off and hardens, leaving behind something new, something that wasn't there before. Destruction and creation all in one movement, forever changing the landscape around it. The world we now walk on was heavily molded, refined, and crafted by massive amounts of lava that flowed from prehistoric volcanoes. It's a little hard to imagine what a world can look like when there are streams of lava all over the place, yet some of the moons in our known galaxy can give us a glimpse of what Earth may have looked like in its infancy. The earth would have been trying to find its way, settling into its new form and trying to get a grip on all the explosive energy just beneath the surface. Honestly, this sounds a bit like how humans grow and get a better grip on their anger. Children just react; they tend not to have filters. Control is something we learn as we see how others respond to our actions. We manage our anger as we grow, and we modify it to become more socially acceptable.

Whether we like to admit it or not, we all pour lava. The solar plexus chakra is our center of magma, and when it builds to the point of breaking, it spills out of us as burning rage, pain, hurt, frustration, excitement, eagerness, and anticipation. But not all outpourings are bad. Remember, lava is both destructor and creator. This is something we truly need to get comfortable with, especially if we want to make changes in our lives.

Not all eruptions in our lives will be because something triggered us in a negative way. If anything, the shapeshifter is here to assist you in learning how to move from aggression to deliberate creation. This mermaid archetype and the power of lava want to show you how to look at your moments of disruption and see them as messages, guides, and portals of fantastic opportunity. But first, we need to change how we see our burning energy and what happens around us as it flows.

When you understand that you are both a conduit and generator of energy, you tend to lean into your personal power. This, in turn, alerts you to when emotions like anger are blocking you from growing, or when excitement turns to overwhelm and paralyzes you. It is interesting that the solar plexus chakra doesn't really know the difference between anger and excitement; it only knows it is building energy and will need to release it in one form or another. It is up to you to be more aware of how you channel that outpouring.

Your conscious awareness will also need to rise around what is left in the wake of your outpouring. It doesn't matter if a lava spill was done with strategic intention or through reactive impulse, the world around you has been changed by it.

The following spell is designed to help you read the signs of what you have created and will help you get more comfortable with allowing your lava to flow.

Spellwork

There may be a piece of you while you've been reading through this chapter that has said more than once, *I don't get very angry about things*. That is perfectly fine. I would invite you to really explore that statement and see if perhaps you are confusing expressing anger with feeling it. But you do not need to focus on anger for this exercise; you can focus on excitement, being energized, or feeling restless; any of these will bring your inner magma to a boil. The story you tell about your feelings isn't as important as the feelings that trigger your solar plexus.

For this spell, which really is just very simple candle magic, all you are going to need is a candle. Because you know what also flows like lava and takes on a new shape once cooled? Wax! I would highly recommend you use a mermaid-shaped candle for this spell; just google mermaid candles and see if you can find a supplier in your local area. If not, a larger pillar candle will be just fine, as long as it is not in glass or contained in any way.

MAGICAL ITEMS

A Large Candle: It's important to see the way the wax melts for this spell, so your candle needs to be big enough to drip wax and your wax needs to be free to form shapes

This spell is honestly one of the easiest you will ever do. Drop your shoulders, relax your jaw, and take a couple of slow, deep breaths in through the nose and out through the mouth. When you feel yourself connected to the moment your body, bring to mind either a situation or person that makes you feel angry. If you are working with feelings of excitement or restlessness, bring that sort of situation to mind. Do not judge this feeling or the conditions that created it; just see it and allow yourself to feel the emotion in your gut.

Take another couple of breaths and light your candle. As you light it, say, "Mermaid shifter I call to thee, show me where I am setting my lava free."

Leave your candle burning for as long as possible, ideally until it burns all the way down. The real magic happens when you see how the wax burns. How is it creating pathways or blocks around the emotion you charged it with?

As you're examining the way the wax burns, be on the lookout for the following:

Clear, Even Burn: This is when the whole candle burns down evenly, at the same time. There don't seem to be any blocks, passages, or rivers of wax. This means you have good control over your emotions in regard to this person or situation. You are not letting your emotions get the better of you, and everything seems to be working to benefit all involved.

Wax in the North: If there seems to be a buildup of wax in this direction, this could mean that you are not listening to your soul voice about this situation/person/problem. You are blocking your inner voice, or you do not trust your intuition. This is not a bad thing; this is merely the shapeshifter letting you know what might be hindering your progress. If, however, you have a clear area facing north and things seem to be flowing nicely, you are doing a good job of taking instruction from your soul voice/higher self.

Wax in the South: A buildup of wax here indicates that how you are feeling is blocking your ability to bring joy into your life. A block in this direction may mean that you have stopped being present in the here and now, instead allowing the past to rob you of the present's joy. If, however, you have wax flowing freely to the south, you are keeping yourself grounded in the present. You make sure all your actions are driven by your immediate needs. This is also a good indicator that you are approaching your issue with playful curiosity and childlike wonder.

Wax in the East: If you notice this side of your candle's wax just doesn't seem to budge, this is an indicator that you are not being flexible with how you are seeing or perceiving a problem, person, or situation. Your wall of wax is letting you know that you have built some pretty big resistance around a new idea, a new way of thinking, a new way of acting, or even a new way of being. This may mean you have totally hooked yourself to a narrative or story about your current emotion, and you aren't willing to create a new one anytime soon. Conversely, if rivers of wax are flowing here and the east is open, then congratulations! New things are on their way, and you are open and ready to receive them.

Wax in the West: Blocks in this direction might mean you aren't willing to seek help or assistance around this issue, feeling, or person. Because you've put up a wall between yourself and those with experience and wisdom, you might be feeling a little isolated (on top of all the other emotions bubbling up from your gut). Dig a little deeper and ask yourself if you feel shame about what you need assistance with, or are you really just that stubborn? Do not pass judgment on yourself; instead, focus on finding a solution. On the contrary, flowing wax in this direction shows how receptive you are; you're open to support. Well done! You allow others to hold space for you and assist you during moments of anger, pain, overwhelm, or excitement.

Over the course of burning your candle, the wax will shift, morph, and change, just like lava. Just like the shapeshifter. Make a note when walls come tumbling down. Consider taking pictures during the burning process and at the end; you could add these to your journal for further exploration.

I enjoy exploring the way my candles burn. In my work with the Goddess, I often see rituals, spells, and prayers as ways in which the Goddess speaks to me. In this case, my candle is the paper, and the wax writes the messages from the Goddess.

Know that your mermaid guide is always speaking to you with love, compassion, and kindness. The shapeshifter only want the very best for you. Take their messages with the energy in which they are given, and allow these messages to mold you into the being you want to be.

Mermaid Connection Exercise: Journaling with the Shapeshifter

I wonder, are you the same person here at the end of the chapter as you were at the beginning? This chapter was about change, transformation, and the many different versions of who you are. You burned with the lava, maybe even getting a little angry as you took action toward your new shapeshifting self. There is no doubt there was a lot to unpack in this chapter. This feels like a good time to crack open your journal and reflect on what you have learned about yourself while working with the shapeshifter.

- Where do you feel you have unresolved anger in your life?
- How are you making space in your life for the new you?
- What sort of consequences are shaping your current reality?

- Where do the different versions of you show up and play?
- What one tip from the shapeshifter will you implement in your daily life?

Answering these prompts is an action. It is using the energy of the solar plexus chakra in a very intentional way. Even if you only answer one prompt, you have engaged your third energy center. These prompts might even have triggered other actions! Allow your thoughts to flow and do your best not to judge them too much. Once you feel complete, move on to the cartomancy work.

Cartomancy: The Fool

The Fool

You have moved beyond the halfway point in your journey with this book, the mermaids, and the phases of the moon. You are now moving out of the bright light and into the shadows yet again. It is time to take a closer look at where you are and how you feel about it. In life, there will be times when you need to reorientate yourself, to check in and make sure your thoughts and feelings are still aligned with the journey you began under the new moon—and honestly, if they aren't, that is okay. But you do need to know either way so you can course correct if need be.

The tarot card alignment for the shapeshifter is the Fool. There is a fluid nature to this card, where outcomes have yet to be established. The journey is the blessing. If you are using an oracle deck, look for a card that has the energy of the child or the wanderer, or even a map.

Place the Fool card or an aligned oracle card faceup in front of you. This is your anchor card, also known as your significator; it grounds the energy of your inquiry and focuses it squarely on the Fool. Pick up the rest of your deck and shuffle. Then, draw three cards and lay them underneath your Fool card.

- Card 1: Feelings; how you feel about where you are right now
- Card 2: Thoughts; how you think about where you are as opposed to where you thought you would be
- Card 3: Next steps; an action you need to take to course correct or get back on track

Do you best not make any judgments about the cards you have drawn. The whole point of this spread is to make space for you to reconnect with your journey, so don't beat yourself up if you have gotten off track. It is normal for things to change—that is kinda the whole theme of this chapter! So maybe it makes sense for your journey to have shapeshifted as well.

This wraps up your time with the shapeshifter. The mermaids and I recommend taking a small break before you dive into the next chapter to allow yourself some integration time. You have done a lot of work, even if it doesn't feel like it, so be kind and gentle to yourself. When you are ready, the mermaids and I shall see you on the next page.

seven

The Nymph

The Universe is a feeling place. It cannot be controlled by force or violence, nor can you yell at it to get your way. The only way to nudge the Universe in the direction you would like it to go is to feel it. I'm going to be honest, I never used to believe this. I thought it was a bunch of New Age, woo-woo nonsense. That was until I decided to do a small experiment.

Before we go any further, I should point out that this chapter isn't just about manifestation; it will be mentioned, but this chapter is also about how your emotional world drives the energy of your physical world. The way it does that is very much dependent on how we are feeling. Not so much how we feel moment to moment, but how we hold on to a feeling, letting it soak into us and hook itself to the way we think, perceive, and ultimately act. Okay, back to my experiment.

In 2011 my wife and I went to a book event in southern California. This particular bookstore did events for some pretty large names, and the place was packed with close to one hundred people at this particular event. The evening was fabulous and we met some very interesting people. As I wandered around the bookstore, browsing the selection of books and decks, one of the decks jumped off the shelf and landed on my foot. This sort of thing happens to me more than it should, to be honest. As I picked the deck up, I knew it was a sign that one day I was also going to do an event at that bookstore. I ended up buying the deck, and the next day we drove back to our home in Las Vegas.

A few months later my wife and I were back at that same bookstore, and I asked how someone does events in their space. We spoke to the manager and got all the paperwork, and I knew I was going to have an event there very soon. And I did. But it was a disaster—no one showed up. Rightly so! My event title sucked and I was very much a nobody in the literary world. But I stood in the middle of that empty room, closed my eyes, and allowed myself to imagine it being full. I leaned all the way into this vision, feeling how it would feel to teach to a room full of eager attendees. I held that vision and all the feelings for around fifteen minutes. I mean, I had paid for the room—I was at least going to get some use out of it! Then we left. I felt so confident about coming back to that bookstore that I left feeling more energized than when I went in.

Fast forward three years. I was working on my very first tarot deck, *Animal Totem Tarot*, and I was back in that bookstore holding a workshop with my wife in a sold-out room. I was still a nobody, as I did not have any publications under my belt except a self-published book, and no one in that room had read it. But I had a fantastic class and I was in the vortex of becoming somebody. My vision that I held three years earlier had come to pass. It was exactly how I had imagined it. The feeling and energy of the room was identical to the one I had leaned into for fifteen minutes. I created this event at that moment; I have no doubt about it.

Oh, and to further prove that it was all connected, the deck that jumped off the shelf and landed on my foot that day was a deck of angel cards. I had only just started my journey with the angels at the time. The event I sold out three years later was about angels. Coincidence? No. It was absolutely a sign to have faith and keep holding space for that vision no matter what. Everything that happened to bring that vision to life is what this chapter is all about: the playful energy of the nymph, the grounding and balancing of the last quarter moon, the emotional power of the sacral chakra, and the deep abundance of the lake. You need all of these elements to make a dream come true. You need to have fun, choose a destination, feel it and then allow it to rise to the surface.

Something to keep in mind as you move through the exercises in this chapter: these types of goals are long-term. It took over three years for me to pull my vision off. Everything you will learn and do in this chapter is about setting you up for the long game. Think of it as sending a fabulous surprise gift to your future self. You have no idea when it will arrive, you just know it will.

Mermaid Archetype: Nymph

The energy of the nymph is a subtle one, and it can be easy to miss when walking through the world. The nymph will speak to you on the breeze and send you messages in the form of leaves, pine cones, or acorns. They will often point out your next direction by the way the rain sweeps across the land. Wherever you live, the nymph will be communicating with you through your local environment, for they are connected to place, and place is where you live, grow, thrive, and reside. Where there is water, there is life, and where this is life, there will be nymphs.

Modern humans do not think about place as much as our ancestors did, nor do we spend much time in devotional practice with the deities of place in order to maintain and sustain the environment around us. There is very little emotional connection to the spaces we live in, and this is starting to impact the entire planet. The nymph is the activist of the Mermaid Pantheon, for they are the ones who oversee all spaces and places, including the ones destroyed for greed and profit. The nymphs are seeing the devastating effects of climate change up close and personal as old forests burn, waterholes dry up, lakes become polluted due to fracking, and extreme weather patterns bring increased flooding.

The nymphs are here to show us that how we feel collectively ends up creating the world we all experience. Right now the world seems to be suffering, and humanity right alongside it. Yet that would only be half the story. You see, part of the activism the nymphs are in charge of is one of hope, solutions, and a future where we all get to live happily ever after. This isn't toxic positivity; this is just the other half of the coin. Nothing is ever all one thing. Where there is a problem, there is always going to be a solution. We might not like it, but it is there all the same. It is the nymphs' job to show both sides, to keep one foot in the problem and the other foot in the solution. They show us how to bring balance to a world that looks very one-sided.

Now, trying to fix the whole world might seem a little too much for one mere mortal, but the truth is, you were only ever meant to govern your own personal world anyway. When we become devotional stewards to our own lives and care for our own small place, this sends a ripple effect to the greater environment. The more people who return to their own place and take up the mantle of care, harmony, and love, the more the planet will heal. That is the lesson of the nymph: see where you are right now as your personal place of activism. Protect it, care for it, and make sure it is healthy and thriving.

It is time to bring forth your inner nymph. Free your inner guardian of place and allow them to start cleaning up and reenergizing your current living environment. Even if you feel like you have it pretty well handled, there are always aspects that can be improved. There are always blind spots in our lives, places we don't want to look at, times we avert our gaze. When we call forth the power and magic of the nymph, we can no longer look away.

Remember, when you are working with this archetype you have one foot in the problem and one foot in the solution. You will need to remain balanced and nonjudgmental; look for outcomes that benefit all involved. This is easier said than done, but your nymph guide, a guide we all have access to, understands this and asks you to be gentle with yourself as you learn to deepen your connection to your inner nymph energy. Take it slow and keep it small. The nymph does not try to solve big problems; rather, they focus on the smaller problems that contribute to big issues, the problems that get missed or left behind because the larger, louder areas of life drown them out.

Devotional Practice

You have a decision to make right here, right now. You must decide which of your worlds needs you to step up and connect to place. For the sake of this book, you have two options: your home or your workplace. (If you happen to work from home, then your workplace would be your office.) You must pick just one. Keep in mind that the nymph focuses on the small things in order to impact the larger parts of life. This means you have to think small in order to have big results. So, which of your worlds needs you to reconnect with it? Make the decision now.

Next, grab your journal. Do some automatic writing with your nymph guide. Use the following journal prompts as a guide to see what information you can receive. The best way to work with these prompts is to write whatever comes to mind. Do not try to make sense of it as you write it, and do not make claims about its truth until after your journal session is complete. It is important to stay connected to the flow of thoughts as they come to the surface. You will have time to edit, dissect, or even explore further after you've allowed your brain's responses to spill onto the page. It is entirely up to you how you wish to approach these prompts. Sometimes it is helpful to set a timer for each prompt so you know you only have a set period of time to get your answer down. Do whatever feels best for you. The most important thing is that you work through each prompt.

- How have I allowed myself to disconnect from this space?
- When do I disconnect, and what situations tend to trigger this separation?
- Where have I been focused on in this area of my life: the problem or the solution?
- How has this single-minded focus affected my environment?
- What emotions am I feeling when I enter this place, and why does this place make me feel this way?

Once you have all of your thoughts on the page, it is time to see where in your world you can bring a deeper feeling of balance and connection. Perhaps you want to bring more gratitude to your home/workplace and all it does for you; this might look like sending healing energy to your home or place of work every morning as you wake up. Perhaps you want to feel more in harmony with your surroundings; this might look like donating or throwing away old, unwanted things that have a negative emotion attached to them. We often hold on to items others have given us even when they are filled with emotions other than joy. In order to heal your environment and set it up for growth, you may very well need to do a good clean out.

When you have decided on your course of action, make a commitment to do this devotional work for at least thirty-three days. This will assist you in deepening your connection to your inner nymph and allows you integration and restoration time as well.

Moon Phases: Last Quarter

Under the last quarter moon, it is time to restore a certain amount of balance and harmony to your life. Since the full moon, you have been burning energy. More than likely, your mind has been very focused on one part of your life. Now you must shift your focus by broadening it; bring the whole picture into focus. See which areas you have been neglecting and make a plan to restore balance to them slowly. Balance isn't as simple as trying to give equal attention or time to things; balance is more about energy and awareness. Your mind and body will only give attention to the parts of your life that you have defined as important, yet there are other aspects of your everyday life that need you to be aware of them and direct energy toward them every so often. This is the sort of balance we are talking about here, under the watchful gaze of the last quarter moon. Zoom out on your daily activities and give yourself permission to explore what else is happening in your life. Take time to see if your priorities have changed or if people have entered or left your life. Oftentimes we don't take time to acknowledge relationship exchanges, but this moon is ideal for that sort of work.

Nymphs are observers of place, meaning they are constantly reviewing the space they inhabit. They can sense subtle changes and are aware of how all the pieces move together to create the whole. The pieces of your life may have shifted since the new moon, yet you may be unaware of how they have moved and what that movement means. Ask the nymph to ground you into place and reconnect you to the spaces where you live, work, and play. Allow the nymph to tether you so you can dive deep into these places and explore them. Do this as an observer. Remember, your job under this particular moon phase is to restore some balance and some harmony, not to judge what is or what has been. Being able to simply explore with curiosity is a gift because it allows you to sit with what is and to see what is working, where connections are flowing, and where the threads have dropped or broken. This space also releases you from making rash emotional decisions. Instead, you can just focus on asking the question *Will this bring me a feeling of balance and harmony?* Then you can take actions that bring this line of inquiry into being.

Here under the last quarter moon, you are finding what balance and harmony mean as you head away from the light. What kind of balance will the shadows bring? How will releasing the light allow more harmony into your life? There is also an opportunity here to contemplate what it means to feel emotionally at ease with the increased darkness. Although the energy of this moon may feel passive, this is an active moon cycle—you are constantly adjusting your actions based on the desire to bring more balance and harmony into your life. The level of awareness you must have during this moon phase is also very active. There is no room for you to be lazy or fall into bad habits under this moon phase; if you do, you won't be able to maintain your big picture focus. When one drifts back into habitual behavior, their focus narrows and they aren't even aware that they have started to block parts of their lives from the conscious mind. So do not be fooled by this moon phase—this is an active and engaged energy, and it will require you to play your part.

Remember that everything you are seeing and feeling under this moon is a direct result of where you have been, what you have created, and the events that led to the full moon. The question you get to ask yourself now is *Where do I want to go?* As the light fades, it is time to think about what's next. What do you want to experience and why? The last quarter moon gives you the room you need to refine your next moves. This is why you need to widen your lens of perception: the path of the future, the path to the new moon, is out of the scope of the past.

An ever-adjusting focal point is needed to chart your next course. The map you need to read is the one that comes next, and the best time to start the next phase of your journey is when you feel in harmony with the move. In energy work, we would call this balancing a time of integration, a space that allows you to assess, absorb, and attune. This is why you want to allow the nymph to ground you, bring you back to center, and plant you firmly in the here and now. Allow the nymph to wash away the tracks that have led you here and to clear the way for what is to come.

Place your hands over your pelvis. Gently close your eyes and take a deep, steadying breath. Drop your shoulders and let the tension of where you have been drop away from you. Take another slow inhale and bring in new energy. Exhale to a place of balance. Let your breath bring you back to center, over and over again.

Call the nymph to you and ask them to reset, restore, and balance your body, mind, and emotions. Feel the nymph's energy wash over you from the top of your head to the tips of your toes. Hold this energy for a few more breaths, then drop your hands and open your eyes. Take a good look around. What do you need to adjust and bring back into harmony?

Ritual: A Call for Harmony

I feel it is important to point out that harmony is not necessarily peace. Even though these two tend to be tied together in requests and magical petitions, it could be said that peace is a by-product of harmony. It is important to understand what harmony is before asking the nymph for it. Harmony is when different things come together and create something beautiful. In music it is when different instruments play together in a way that creates an enticing song. In life it may be having moving parts working together to bring about your goal. For the purpose of this ritual, harmony is when the Goddess blesses you with divine flow. In divine flow, all the moving pieces in your life seem to drop into place without any real effort on your part; they just seem to magically work together in a well-choreographed dance.

Lots of things have moved and shifted since the last new moon, and certainly since the full moon. Finding balance will require harmony and bringing all the pieces back together—especially all the pieces of you. Over the course of the lunar month, you have fragmented your energy. You have cast pieces of yourself into the wind, and now it is time to call them home. Call them forth so you can now be in harmony with yourself.

MAGICAL ITEMS

A Candle: Use an orange candle for the sacral chakra or a pink candle for the heart; you can even use both to symbolize harmony in action

Light your candles and get comfortable. Sit on a meditation mat if you have one.

Place your right hand on your heart and your left hand over your sacral chakra, in the middle of your pelvis. Focus the breath through the heart and imagine sending it down into the sacral chakra area. Take slow, steady breaths in and out the nose. Let them become rhythmic as you drop into a more relaxed state.

When you feel yourself in harmony with your body, call forth your nymph guide. Ask them to gather the pieces of you that will be required to bring harmony into your life—the pieces that have been scattered across time, space, and dimensions—and bring them home to you.

Close your eyes while you allow the nymph to do their work. Just focus on your breathing. You may see these pieces of yourself as colors, or you may feel them as different energies all coming together at the heart as you inhale and dropping down to the sacral chakra as you exhale. Continue doing this until you feel complete, or until your nymph guide lets you know there are no more pieces to gather.

Thank your nymph guide and drop your hands. Allow yourself a few more slow, deep breaths as you integrate this new energy. When you feel ready, blow out your candle(s) and move on with the rest of your day.

You can do this ritual as often as you like, especially during moments where you really feel the need to bring harmony into your life. Remember, you do not need to wait until the last quarter of the moon to do this; you can bring this energy into your daily life at any time. If you do repeat this ritual, you can relight the original candle(s) and keep them just for this ritual. Nymphs like the idea of having special candles for special work, as it anchors you to place through that act of ritual.

Energetic Alignment: Sacral Chakra

Let's go back in time to when I used to teach meditation classes. It was well over a decade ago. Back then, I used to do a meditation called "Fishing in Sacral Lake." How funny that here I am all these years later, revisiting the sacral chakra and the energy of the lake in a book about mermaids! Never in a million years would I have envisioned that this book would be the thing that brought me back to that time and those teachings. But here we are. Unlike my small class in Las Vegas, this book will touch more people globally, so I had better make sure I swim straight with this chapter!

I am always in awe of how creative energy works. It flows into our lives and connects us to moments in time. Then again, this is the chakra where our memories are stored, so I guess it really should not be that surprising. The sacral chakra has a depth to it that is very different from other major chakra points, for this one is personal. It changes from person to person. I have found that the more you dive into the lake, the deeper it gets. The energies of the sacral chakra seem bottomless to those who activate their center of creation on a regular basis.

Before we go further, let's define creative energy. There is always an assumption that creativity equates to artistic endeavors, which is factually incorrect. Yes, those in the arts do use their center of creation a lot, but so do parents, engineers, software developers, traders, and every other problem-solver on the planet. For me, creative energy is about being in the flow of solutions. This is where creative energy shines, expands, and adds depth to your second chakra. The people who focus on solutions are not the same as people who focus on problems. Solution-based people are seeking movement and flow, and they are driven to create resolution in their endeavors. Problem-orientated people are stuck and limited, and they allow memories about similar problems to dictate the terms of their lives. Nymphs are solution-oriented, as they take their life cues from nature itself. And the natural world always finds a way. Without fail, nature will always find a solution. So will your second chakra, if you allow it.

Your second chakra is a solution-based energy point. It needs to create solutions, and oftentimes it uses emotional memory to do so. It seeks out other times you were in the flow of solving problems and creating new ways to move, grow, and expand and draws on that feeling of purpose, satisfaction, and desire. These emotions are part of what expands your second chakra, adding depth to your lake. The more desire, purpose, and satisfaction you create in your life, the happier your second chakra will be.

And if your second chakra is happy, you are blissfully happy. It is only when we allow ourselves to get tangled up in the reeds and start letting our mind become bogged down in the problem that we start to suffer. The past lives in this energy center, so it is your job to make sure that areas of the past you do not wish to revisit do not get stirred up and muddy your creative waters. Once your water gets dirty, it becomes hard to see where you are going, which leads you to doubt and fear, and before you know it, you are just swimming in circles.

Your creative energy is also inspired by where you live and the environment you find yourself in. Nymphs are intrinsically connected to place, and they use it to nourish and nurture them. This means your sacral chakra is also very influenced by place when it is seeking solutions. So, is your space and place feeding you? How is your space adding to your creative energy? What small things can you do to make it more inspiring?

Not all of us can (or should) change where we live. However, we can infuse our homes, offices, and spaces with things that make us feel connected, alive, and passionate. For me, it is plants, trees, and water. My wife and I live in the desert, far, far away from any body of water. It is also pretty darn barren in the desert. We have solved this by living in the one part of town that is covered with trees. We are surrounded by parkland and native pines. Our patio and our house are filled with plants; we have plants everywhere, not in a jungle type of way, but in a calm and relaxing way. Our apartment is situated across from the pool. We can watch the sun setting between two giant palms over the water every single night. The desert is never going to be the beach or the forest, but we have done our very best to live in a place that ticks all of our boxes to the best of its abilities! Ever since we moved here, we have noticed a complete shift in our lives. You could say we discovered depths we had yet to explore!

Now you know a little more about how your second chakra works with the Mermaid Pantheon. You need to be focused on solutions and steer clear of problems. You've also learned that place is magical, and you can call on your nymph guide or your own inner nymph to create a space that fills you up, makes you passionate about life, and nourishes and inspires you. All of this will assist you in rebalancing, restoring, and returning yourself to a place of calm under the watchful light of the last quarter moon.

Healing Exercise

It has been over ten years since I first taught this particular meditation. The interesting thing is that I have changed some of the ways I work with the second chakra, which means that this meditation is not the same as the one I taught back in 2009. Instead, it's an upgraded version, a version that is more aligned with the new technology of the sacral chakra that has been revealed to me over the last twelve months. Right now, in this moment in human history, we need to look for different things inside the second chakra to spark creation. We need to move into the flow of solutions and allow ourselves freedom from the past; we need to unhook ourselves from generational judgment. So go ahead and get comfortable—we are about to take a trip to Sacral Lake.

You can do this meditation in a yoga position, lying down, or in a nice comfortable seat. Choose wherever you will be the most calm and peaceful. Once you have found your spot, take a couple of slow, deep breaths, inhaling through the nose and exhaling through the mouth. Let the shoulders drop. Relax the jaw as you give your body permission to rest, stop, and pause. Let the mind relax as well; allow all of your thoughts to just float on through. Do not hook to any of them. Breathe and drop into this moment. You can continue with your eyes open, or you can go ahead and close them. Continue to breathe slowly and deeply, lengthening the inhale and exhale, letting the breath guide your level of relaxation.

As you sink into this moment, imagine yourself sitting at the edge of a lake. This lake is somewhere that feels safe, secure, and stable to you. Your lake will not look like everybody else's; it is unique in its size and in the plant life around it, as well as in the environment in which it sits and its depth. Breathe in and breathe out.

Wherever you find yourself, look to the side. Sitting next to you is a fishing pole. On that pole, you are going to hook your current problem, question, or line of inquiry, whatever that may be. Put it on the hook and then cast that hook into Sacral Lake. This problem is your bait, and it is going to attract a solution, answer, or some other form of guidance. The solution could be from your personal past; it could be an answer given to you from an ancestor or family member; it could be guidance given to you from a different timeline. Regardless of where it comes from, receive it without judgment.

Sit calmly on the bank of the lake and wait for your solution. Once you have movement on your line and your solution has bitten down on your problem, it is time to reel it in. How you reel this in will give you an indication on how resistant you are to the solution, guidance, or answer: If reeling it in is a battle of epic proportions and you find yourself fighting with your line, this is your level of resistance to seeking some sort of solution to your current problem. If, however, your line comes up with ease and grace and you just slip that solution right out of the water and put it into the bucket next to you, you are ready to change. You are more open and willing to move into thriving and growing.

Once you have your solution in your bucket, put your line down and find a new place to settle down with that bucket. Really explore what's inside. Do your best to memorize whatever you can about it. Whether there are words, colors, lights, objects, symbols, or something else, take a snapshot with your mind's eye so that you can journal about it later. When you have gotten all of the information that you require (or all that is possible right now), scoop that solution back into your bucket, walk back to the edge of the lake, and throw it back in. This is definitely a catch-and-release type of scenario. You just never know when that solution may be needed again.

Give thanks to the lake. Honor it by touching your heart and reciting five gratitude statements, then sit back down and focus on the breath coming back to your body. Come back to the space that surrounds you, breathing in through the nose and out through the mouth. Roll out your shoulders, stretch your neck, and wiggle your fingers and toes. When you are ready, open your eyes if you had them closed. If your eyes were already open, blink a few times. Then reach for your journal and write down as much as you can about the problem, the solution, and the next five actions you will take to be in harmony with the nymph.

Place of Power: Lake

If you have been reading this chapter from the beginning, then you will not be surprised that we are still mucking about with lakes. However, if you are one of those chapter jumpers or you are using this book for your bibliomancy practice, surprise! We are talking about lakes!

There are people who absolutely adore lakes. Lots of people like walking around a lake or picnicking lakeside, and of course, let us not forget partying on the lake in a boat. I honestly don't think I realized what a big deal lakes were until I moved to the US. I had never heard anyone in Australia get excited to go to a lake. Down Under, we're beach people. This could be because I grew up during the beginning of extreme drought in Australia. Fifty years later, the rest of the world is catching up to the water conditions of my youth.

Needless to say, I have never personally been much of a lake person. Since moving to the US, I have visited many lakes. Some are human-made, like the couple that are driving distance from my home in Las Vegas, though they are drying up fast. The other lakes I've seen were made by nature in Oregon, North Carolina, and upstate New York. I have visited enough of them to know that I am not a lake person. That does not mean I cannot learn from the lake. It does not mean that the wisdom of the lake is not aligned with me and my journey. If anything, because I am not a fan of the lake, this more than likely means it has the most to teach me.

There is a bit of a misconception in the New Age community that if something is not "aligned," then you are meant to ignore it or walk away from it. I have seen it happen with some of my business clients, and I have seen it in those who want to enter publishing. This way of thinking is extremely short-sighted and will cause you to miss opportunities that could very well change your life in the most miraculous and magical ways. The biggest gift the mermaids have given me over the last few years has been showing me that just because I don't like something doesn't mean it won't bring massive value to my life. So, if you are like me and lakes are not your favorite place in the world, stay with the lessons in this chapter, as you need them the most.

A lake is a body of water that is completely surrounded by land. Small lakes are called ponds, and larger lakes can become seas. The Caspian Sea is actually the world's biggest lake. Although rivers and creeks can flow into the lake, unless there is a flood of some kind, nothing flows out. Everything is contained with nowhere to go. Lakes are like the end of the road for water. Maybe that's why I don't like them: they feel restricted and limited. Yet, there are times in our lives when we need to enforce our boundaries—times when we need to contain our energy, thoughts, and emotions so we can focus on healing or growth. Limits can be a very good thing when used correctly.

Within the confines of the lake, a very unique ecosystem develops, one that you will not find in moving bodies of water. A lentic ecosystem—which is found in lakes, ponds, and some wetland areas—can only be created in stillness. This means there are certain plants and animals that can only live in a calm, peaceful, still environment. If we apply this to ourselves, there are parts of our mind, emotions, and physical being that can only exist when everything around is perfectly still. That is powerful.

At the time of writing this book, the world was in the middle of a pandemic. Rolling lockdowns have just swept the planet. Collectively we were asked to limit, constrain, and restrict ourselves. Not everyone was able to do this in a peaceful, calm, or even a willing way. We have seen firsthand how difficult it is for postmodern humanity to bring itself to stillness. Some even protested for their right to movement. Yet, funnily enough, many of these same people do not see the right of movement for refugees, minorities, or even those in desperate poverty. As a whole, most

Western societies have become addicted to instant gratification, constant streams of information, and ongoing entertainment. I often wonder if there is a correlation between the lakes of the world drying up and our inability to stay still. If the world really is a mirror of those who inhabit it, then what is the world currently saying about us as a collective species? And more to the point, can we stop and listen to course correct in time?

I stated earlier in this chapter that the nymph is the activist of the Mermaid Pantheon, so it should not surprise you that the lessons of the lake may have bigger global implications. Remember, we cannot change the whole world, nor should we look to solve massive global problems from our limited standpoint. This brings us full circle to the nymph's connection to place. The lake and the nymph hold the key to gaining clarity about how we can make a larger impact without feeling overwhelmed. We do this by drawing inward, setting firm boundaries, and learning how to tap into the unique and magical ecosystem of our inner stillness, our own personal lake.

Spellwork

For this section I am going to offer you two spells instead of one. You may perform spell one before you do spell two, or you can jump straight to spell two if you already feel good about how you create stillness in your life. The reason I have included two spells is that not everyone who reads this book is going to be in the same place on their journey. Some will have been meditating for years and won't find being still or dropping into the depths of their personal lake difficult or challenging, whereas some of you will be new to just about everything we have covered in this chapter. That being said, even those among us who are seasoned meditators sometimes need a reminder to return to center, as we all experience phases in our life where we will be scattered, disconnected, and unable to navigate our daily lives.

Spell 1: Calling In the Stillness

Before you start this spell, take a moment to make sure you are somewhere you will not be interrupted. You may want to be somewhere quiet, though if you wish to put on some music like a mantra or a calming instrumental track, that is fine.

MAGICAL ITEMS

A Blue Candle: This represents the water of the lake; if you cannot find a blue candle, white will do

An Empty Jar with a Lid: Make sure this has a tight seal

Pen: To write on your sticky notes

Sticky Notes: Any color or size will work

Once you are comfortable, grab your sticky notes and pen. Think of all the tasks, goals, or daily things that you feel have scattered your energy or disrupted your ability to be still. We all have things in our lives that seem to pull us in different directions; now is the time to identify them and write them down.

You are going to write one of these distractions on the first sticky note, using the following structure: "I am calling back the part of myself that [distraction that has been pulling your focus, energy, or emotions]." For example, "I am calling back the part of myself that gets lost in admin work, which makes my mind race."

Or "I am calling back the part of myself that has been consumed by my family's drama."

Use a new sticky note for each distraction. As you finish each note, fold it and place it inside your jar. Keep going until you have run out of things to write about. Once you are done, place the lid on your jar and close it, containing all your requests in one place.

Next, pick up your candle. Write "I am calling me back" on it. You can write this sentence using your pen, your finger, or a carving tool. Then hold your candle to your heart and say "I am calling me back" three times.

Hold the candle over the lid of your jar and light the bottom of the candle. Let the wax drip and melt onto the top of the lid, then push the candle onto the jar lid and hold it for a few seconds until the wax firms back up. The wax should safely secure the candle to the lid of the jar.

Once your candle is secured, it is time to light the candle's wick and activate your spell. As you light the candle, say the following:

I call on the power of the nymph
Connect me to this place
Bring me back
All of me
Across all time, space, and dimension
Bring me back to this place
Contain me to this space
To this time
So I can be still
Make me a lake
Calm

Motionless
Deep
From where I have been
Let me now see
The magic that lies within
This petition is now done

It is important to allow the candle to burn all the way down, so make sure you do this spell when you have the time to watch over your burning flame. If you want to deepen this spell, allow yourself to sit in silence for a few minutes and just watch the flame of your candle. Embodying the stillness you requested will bring it to you sooner rather than later.

Once the candle has burned out, notice how your energy shifts and changes over the next few days. You might find you need more sleep initially as you reintegrate the parts of yourself, but then you should notice a sense of calm, and the need to move your focus outside of yourself won't be nearly as intense.

Spell 2: Connecting to the Magic of the Inner Lake

The point of this spell is to connect you to the unique ecosystem of your inner lake. No one on the planet will have the same living things in their lake that you have in yours. Cool, huh? This is one of the reasons differences are such a fantastic thing. Differences need to be embraced! We are all human, but we are so vastly different, and your inner lake's ecosystem is just one example of this.

This spell is actually a bit of bathtub magic. I am a sucker for bathtime rituals, but do not despair if you are more of a shower person. You can do this ritual in the shower as well, though you will have to put your feet over the drain. You want to be in a contained, lake-like environment, hence the bathtub. You could also sit in the bathtub without putting water in it; just have a basin or glass of water with you. The only thing that cannot be compromised is that you need to use water that is fresh and clean. No soap, salts, bubbles, or herbs can be added to the water. Just water. Regardless of whether you are submerging your mermaid self into a nicely filled bath or not, follow the instructions below.

Stillness is important to this spell, which means both the water and your body need to be still as you recite the words. So if you wanna squirm, do it quickly and then bring yourself to stillness. The only movement should be your breath, which you will inhale and exhale through the nose. Drop the shoulders, unclench the jaw, and breathe deep and slow. Count the inhales to five and exhale to the count of five until you feel yourself slip into that nice, calm, meditative state.

If it is safe to do so, gently close your eyes to limit sensory stimulation. Deepen the breath as you let the outside world completely drop away. Notice the space around you opening up. Feel space behind you, beside you, under you, and above you. Sink deeper into the darkness behind your eyes. When you feel yourself floating slightly, recite the following:

Nymph I am here
Within my lake
Guide me
Show me
The magic that lays beneath
Contained in this place
Designed just for me

Gift to me
What I need
I am open to receive
Right here, right now
For now I understand
The path to freedom
Is here in the limits within

Keep your eyes closed if it is safe to do so. Allow yourself a moment to receive a message, lesson, or gift from your nymph guide. When you feel complete, count from ten to one and open your eyes.

You might find you want to journal after this spell has been cast. If you feel comfortable writing in the tub, go for it. Otherwise, end your water time and start writing, for the spell is now complete.

Mermaid Connection Exercise: Journaling with the Nymph

This has been a very interesting chapter indeed. You have explored your more rebellious self. You've seen parts of who you are wash up on the shores of Sacral Lake, and you have explored the sacredness of the place you live. This feels like a good time to crack open your journal and reflect on what you have learned about yourself while working with the nymph.

- What version(s) of yourself did you need to call back?
- Where do you need to be more of an activist in your own life?
- How does your current environment affect you?

- How can you bring more devotional work into your daily life?
- When do you find yourself feeling creative and in the flow of solutions?

Think of these prompts as a way to start the reflecting process. Do not feel limited by these questions; allow your answers to open up more discussion. Let your thoughts flow freely. There is magic in letting the words spill onto the page. Once you feel complete, move on to the cartomancy work.

Cartomancy: Knight of Pentacles

Knight of Pentacles

There is something slow yet deliberate in the energy of the nymph. Even though it can be turbulent and even troublesome at times, the energy here is akin to the Knight of Pentacles card in a tarot deck. There is a methodical nature to the way the nymph works, moves, and heals. This comes from knowing one's place and space. The Knight of Pentacles can often be seen walking around, taking notes about their current environment. They make it their job to know every coming and going. Nothing is more important to this Knight than maintaining the sacred nature of the place they inhabit. If you are using an oracle deck, a good card to use here would be an earth keeper or land steward—something that has the same sort of energy as the Knight of Pentacles.

Place the Knight of Pentacles card or an aligned oracle card faceup in front of you. This is your anchor card, also known as your significator; it grounds the energy of your inquiry and focuses it squarely on the Knight of Pentacles. Pick up the rest of your deck and shuffle. While you shuffle, think about how you maintain peace, order, and harmony in your life. Then draw three cards.

- Card 1: Where you need to find balance in your life
- Card 2: Where in your life you need to deepen your connection
- Card 3: How you can bring more harmony into your day

This simple spread gives you a very quick snapshot of the energy around your sacral chakra and helps you connect more deeply with your nymph guide.

This wraps up your time with the nymph. The mermaids and I recommend taking a small break before you dive into the next chapter to allow yourself some integration time. You have done a lot of work, even if it doesn't feel like it, so be kind and gentle to yourself. When you are ready, the mermaids and I shall see you on the next page.

eight
The Sprite

It is time to get back to basics. Here at the end of the your journey with the merfolk, strip everything away and then see what is necessary. No fluff, no fuss, just the bare essentials. The energy of the sprite is a simple one; it doesn't need you to add anything to it. Yet, simple doesn't always equate to easy. How many times have you tried to simplify your life, only to make it more complicated? This is why we all need a little sprite energy in our lives. The sprite is a beacon of hope that our everyday existence can be simple and fulfilling. Instead of disconnecting from our lives, we want to deepen the connection we have to daily life and the people in it through the act of simplification.

Modern humans have done a fantastic job of overcomplicating life; it is one of the things we excel at. We have moved from having what we need to get by to things we must have to satisfy the ego. Now, I am not saying wanting things is bad, but there is a difference between having something that is meaningful and something that is just there to provide temporary satisfaction.

The sprite moves too fast to care about collecting trophies for the ego. Organizing consultant Marie Kondo is a great example of sprite energy, and her work is a good example of the essence of the simple nature the sprite brings to our lives. That is pretty much what this chapter is: a Marie Kondo session for your mermaid soul. You'll sort through what surrounds you until you find the meaning in it all, but in a fun and curious way.

This chapter is meant to make you think about what is really important to you hour-to-hour and what you need to thrive. When we talk about going back to basics, the mermaids are not suggesting that you leave yourself with no pleasure or joy. This is not about merely surviving, but about truly finding meaning in your life and in your "stuff." Most people would be surprised by how little they need to thrive and would more than likely not believe how little they need to feel free. Yet freedom, playfulness, and not being weighed down is exactly what your energy body desires.

Your root chakra has a default setting of survival; this setting hasn't changed since early humans lived in caves. This is one of the reasons most of us overindulge or get caught up in keeping up, comparing ourselves to strangers on social media or needing to have the right makeup, clothes, shoes, car, or whatever comparison item you must have to feel connected to the world around you—we think this is what surviving means in our current world. The mermaids, especially the sprite, want to reprogram your root chakra to its "thrive" setting and bring a sense of fulfillment into your life, one that relies less on gathering and more on being. The sprites want to show you how to do this in the most fun way possible. So let's dive in!

Mermaid Archetype: Sprite

The sprite is a water deity that reminds us that life on this paradox of a planet was always meant to be fun. We tend to take things a little too seriously for a temporary existence. The sprite connects us back to the energies we came into this life with: curiosity, wonder, and the excitement of discovering what's next. It is interesting that as we get older, we start to fear all of those things, especially the "what comes next" energy that the sprite swirls into our lives. After a certain age, humans tend to want to know exactly what's going to happen in their future. They want some guarantees that nothing is going to disrupt their lives. Yet children are always looking for the next new thing, creating wondrous worlds filled with imagination. This is what the sprite offers us: that childlike energy. The sprite connects us back to the imagination that is instinctive to us all.

This energy may challenge some of you, as not every adult can unhook themselves from some of the issues and concerns in this chapter, like safety, security, stability, and survival. The four S's tend to trigger another S, stress. But that is kind of the point of the energy of the sprite: to not let the stress creep in. They want to plug you back into the natural supply of the world you live in.

Just like with the crown chakra, there is an element of trust here at the root—trust in spirit, god, goddess, the Universe, or whatever you want to call the cosmic force. The sprite has no trust issues, which is why they can enjoy their experience. Can you say the same? Really letting go and enjoying life isn't always easy in adulthood. It should be, but it tends not to be. We get tied up in knots thinking about the things we "should" be doing or worrying how others might view us. We become guarded, resistant, and, before we know it, we are nothing but stressed-out balls of burnout.

When this happens, we ignore the energy of the sprite, or worse, we lose the ability to identify it at all. Now, let's get clear about something here: embracing sprite energy does not mean you become frivolous or irresponsible. It in no way means you stop doing all the things that make you an adult. Quite the opposite! The sprite wants to show you how to have fun adulting and how to enjoy all the freedoms being a grown-up has gifted you—the big one being not having to ask for permission to do, well, anything!

In my coaching company, I work with a lot of women who are still waiting for someone to give them permission to live, grow, and thrive. It's as if they traded their parents in for stricter guardians called Society. We all do this at some point in our lives. We hold ourselves back, stunt our personal or professional selves, and shackle ourselves to a list of excuses. The sprite is here to remind you that this is all an illusion. You are a free being and you get to choose what you do, when you do it, and how you want to enjoy it. You are the ruler of your king/queen-dom. Lead, laugh, love, and live on your terms.

The sprite is waiting for you to unroll the map of your adventure. It wants to help you chart your course. It's time to decide where you will explore next and who you are going to take with you. In tarot, the Magician card is the embodiment of this sprite energy. The Magician is faith-filled and always ready with a bag of tricks; he traipses through the tarot world filled with excited anticipation because he knows it is already everything it needs to be. This is what the sprite offers you, if you are willing to receive it: A new way of looking at your adult self. A way of reconnecting you to the freedom of choice. A life that is yours, just waiting for you to jump in and take a chance.

Devotional Practice

If you are a tarot nerd like myself, you can use the Magician card for this exercise. Remove it from your deck and place it on your altar or somewhere you can see it on a daily basis. If you are not really into tarot, that is fine; google images of sprites and use one of those instead. All that really matters is that you have a visual image that connects you to the energy of the sprite each and every day for at least seven days. I always encourage my clients to take on a devotional practice of thirty-three days, but the length of time you do this is honestly up to you.

Once you have your image, be it the Magician card or a nice sprite image, set it up where you can see it. Pick up your journal and a pen and just stare at your image. Take a couple of deep, slow breaths in through the nose and let yourself form a connection to the energy of the sprite. You might feel a tingling in your body or hands, or you may just sense that you have connected with this energy. If you feel nothing, do not worry—the sprite is there with you even if you cannot physically feel it.

Now that you have your connection established, open your journal and write at the top of the page: *Today I give myself permission to.* Then just write whatever comes up. You may find you write the above prompt more than once during your journal time; consider writing the prompt at least ten times and filling in the rest of the sentence. Let me give you some examples:

- Today I give myself permission to get all my work tasks done and then go have fun with my partner.
- Today I give myself permission to save some money and spend some money on something that brings my heart joy.

- Today I give myself permission to celebrate a personal win with friends.
- Today I give myself permission to slow down and rest.
- Today I give myself permission to get outside in the sun and away from my desk.
- Today I give myself permission to let go of my worries of the future and enjoy what is in front of me.

Once you've finished writing, put your journal away and go about your day. Repeat this exercise for at least seven days. You might find that the more days you do this, the more things you are giving yourself permission to do—which is rather the point. You are free. You have choices. *You get to make the rules.* This is your one unique and glorious life, and this devotional practice to the sprite will fill up the well of thriving energy deep in your soul.

Moon Phases: Waning Crescent

There is a playful nature to this particular moon phase. It may not be overly active nor passive, but if you allow the energy of the sprite to lead you, this moon phase might just bring a smile to your face and a swing to your step.

By the time this moon phases comes around, you have already had a full month of activities. You have had wins both big and small. You have had things go wrong and possibly even had to adjust your expectations. All in all, you have been through a full cycle of push and pull, expand and contract energy. That is why you get to kick off your shoes and play under the darkening moon. This is the time to wind down. Take a step back and allow some space between you and all those never-ending items on your to-do list. The sprites know that if you can build this habit of playfulness and restoration into your lunar calendar, you won't ever have to worry about burnout ever again. For it is only when we fight natural cycles that we become overly tired, worn out, and a little frayed at the emotional seams. Even if you have had an incredible month where everything that could go right did, you need some downtime. The body doesn't know the difference between good and bad stress; it just knows stress and does its best to combat it. This is why adding this moon phase to your calendar as a monthly reminder to play, find joy, and pamper yourself is vitally important.

It is interesting that this particular moon phase doesn't get a lot of attention. Everyone hypes up the full moon and the new moon, but the waning crescent is deeply and profoundly underrated. (It is my hope that by the end of this chapter, you will agree with me.) It is no mistake that people are attracted to the two moon phases with the biggest amount of drama. I mean, they capture everyone's attention and are impossible to miss in the night sky; one shines so brightly and one doesn't shine at all. But the waning crescent is like the calm before a storm. It is the small gap where you can take a breath, stretch, and tease your toes with some fresh air. As someone who identifies as a high achiever, I know only too well how easy it is to forget to take a moment for oneself—to just stop and do nothing important for five seconds. Life can be a bit of a treadmill: Always somewhere to be. Always something to do. Always people to please. If we're not careful, we can get lost in the noise of the busy work that becomes our lives. This is why I love and adore the sacred two-and-a-half days this moon phase brings. It is the perfect amount of time to just chill, eat ice cream, watch Netflix, and catch up on some reading. If we can't take two days a month to relax and play, then what is the point of this physical existence?

The sprite archetype connects us back to childhood. Children are creative and never stop to question all the incredible places their imagination takes them. The sprite reminds us of the way we used to get lost in the moment. There is safety in this sort of play, something grounding and earthly about reconnecting to that part of us that longs to be free and wild once again. The sprite knows how to connect us back to those primal moments. They reintroduce us to the parts of us that love to lie on the grass and look up at the clouds. Do you ever look at the clouds and notice they look like an animal? That is your inner sprite. That is how they like to bring you back down to earth—by helping you marvel at the magic that surrounds you. Throw in the mysterious nature of the darkening moon and you have a party!

The energy of the sprite is something you can invite into your life or something you can embody. It is your choice. There is no wrong or right way to work with the sprite under this particular moon phase. Just make sure before you sit down to do your ritual that you know which way you want to work with the sprite. You need to be intentional with your moon work, even if it is playful. So, decide right here and now: will you be embodying the sprite, or will you merely be asking the energy of the sprite to come into your life and show you how to have more fun?

Once you know how you will be working with this energy, you can start to prepare for your ritual. But again, keep in mind that all of this is meant to be fun. Intentional, sure, but don't get hooked on trying to get this "right." If you find yourself overthinking this, you have pushed the magical sprite energy out of your ritual. And that is not at all how we want to proceed.

Instead, drop your shoulders. Relax. Take a deep breath and smile. Now laugh. For no reason whatsoever. Just laugh. Laugh like a lunatic and let the energy flow through you. This is all to prepare your energy for the ritual. We need to be in the vibrational place of the energy we wish to bring into our lives, so laugh and let your energy rise. It doesn't matter if it is forced or real laughter; the act itself will shift your vibrational body. Smirk, giggle, and wiggle your eyebrows. Get as silly and crazy as you can. Let the sprite energy wash over you like a wave, starting at the top of your head and going all the way down to the tips of your toes. Once you feel this energy move over you, you know you are ready to begin your ritual for the waning crescent!

Ritual: Embracing the Golden Hour

Play is one of the best ways to connect with your body, the moment you are in, and the environment that surrounds you. Schedule this particular form of play just before the sun sets. This is the time of day that feels the most aligned to this particular moon phase, and that means you do not have to wait for a waning crescent to do this ritual. This particular time of the early evening is often referred to as the golden hour. The light changes to a specific hue and showers the world in a golden, sparkling, glittering glow. My wife absolutely loves this time of day, and we have spent many an hour dancing on the sand as the water turns to liquid gold just before darkness descends.

This is the time of day that birds fly back to their nests and little creatures scurry back home to stay safe from nighttime predators. There is a natural flow to this time, to this phase. You might already have a ritual for this time of day but just aren't aware of it. Because humans, like nearly all sentient beings, are creatures of habit, it is time for you to observe and study your golden hour ritual.

Over the next week, write down everything you do at this time of the day. Keep track of how you feel and what sort of habits you have created around this time. Notice if your golden hour habits are fun, playful, and grounding. If not, think about ways you can implement the energy of the sprite. Remember, how you do this will depend on whether you have chosen to embody the sprite or call on the energy of the sprite.

Perhaps your new golden hour ritual will be going for a walk around your neighborhood and connecting with your neighbors. If you are fortunate enough to live near a body of water, perhaps your sprite will want to dance with you in the sand as golden beams sparkle across the watery landscape. Or maybe this will be when you settle into your favorite chair with a nice cup of tea and journal about your wildest dreams. All of these are wonderful sprite-based rituals that you can make into habits either during the waning crescent cycle or every evening as the golden hour spreads its magical light. The when, where, and how is totally up to you. Have fun, be creative, and let the energies of the sprite and the moon guide you.

Energetic Alignment: Root Chakra

Let's consider the role of the root chakra in a watery world. It may seem strange to consider the concept of stability when discussing a world that is surrounded by flowing liquid, yet all bodies of water are connected to land. The ocean does have a bottom, and it is solid. The shoreline is solid and earthbound. Rivers and lakes require the earth to hold them and support them so that they can flow, grow, and maintain. Even waterfalls need bodies of earth to flow over. No matter how you cut it, you cannot escape the solid, stable, grounding energy of the root chakra, even in a watery world.

The root chakra is just as important for mermaids as it is for humans. There is no escaping its connection to the physical world or its pull to form matter into something solid. The root chakra is the energy that pumps through the mermaid's tail, giving them the ability to navigate and move through the water they live in. In much the same way, the root chakra pumps energy through human legs, giving us mobility and autonomy.

To be honest, I like adding a bit of flow and flex to the energy of the root chakra. Sometimes it can become fixed, stuck, and unmovable, much like a mountain. When this happens, we can start to feel frustrated, trapped, and disconnected to our lives. Here in the Mermaid Pantheon, we get to wiggle our root chakra energy around a little more freely, for in the water we are more buoyant.

The root chakra is our first point of connection to physical experience. It is the first energy center we plug into when we slow down our vibrational energy enough to manifest in a physical form. It is the other side of our chakra battery, its flip side being the crown chakra. This chakra is in charge of how connected we are and the depths of the connections we wish to explore while we live our physical incarnations. Most people understand the concept of connection, but what I have found in my work with private clients and entrepreneurs is that very few people understand the *depth* of connection.

People have become increasingly transactional in their connections with the people and places in their lives. Place no longer means something to most people. They have a house, a job, possibly a family and kids, yet there appears to be little depth to all of these things. Their root chakras are a mess, and there is a total lack of connection in their daily lives. I have been guilty of this in the past, so I know how easy it is for this to happen. It doesn't take much for us to float into a zombie-like life, filled with automatic habits and a sensation of just going through the motions. These are your root chakra red flags, and they are screaming, *Mayday! Mayday! We have a massive connection problem!*

The three things most people want and need from the root chakra are safety, security, and stability. I am always amazed at how few people know what this looks and feels like in their lives. What words they will speak, what stories they will tell, and how they will stay connected to these safe, secure, stable states is not something most people sit and contemplate. Yet this is the "depth" part of connection. You gotta know how to sustain these things in order to achieve them.

Your root chakra has a specific language it uses to let you know when you have achieved a deep connection to your physical experience. You will notice comforting feelings and thoughts around safety, both personal and global. You will be able to make decisions without fear, and you won't be afraid to connect with new people, which is something the sprite loves doing. You will take different actions when your root chakra is empowered and stable, as you will have shifted from surviving to thriving. When security is achieved, you will find yourself willing to take risks, open up to growth, and explore the world around you. When your root chakra is plugged in and turned on, you will be moving that mermaid tail of yours and making waves!

Healing Exercise

We have talked a lot in this chapter about moving from surviving to thriving, mainly because this is the next level for the root chakra. It is time to upgrade your chakra technology and start running a new program. This is not just true for you, dear reader—it is true for all of humanity. The world we live in is not the same as it once was. Things have changed dramatically. Yet, for whatever reason, most of humanity is still running on the same software our prehistoric ancestors were. Can you imagine trying to run computer software from the '90s on your current device??? How would that even work? Our computers get upgraded all the time. New versions of code are constantly being swapped out and exchanged on our tech devices. But for some reason, so many people balk at the idea that our own software might need constant upkeep, clean outs, and upgrades. We all want to feel safe in our skin, regardless of how we identify or what we call ourselves. We all want to love and be loved for who we are, not for who others want us to be. This all starts with upgrading one's energy centers, and it all starts here, in the first one, the root.

Start this meditation by getting as comfortable as you can, preferably in a seated position. Your spine should be straight and the base of your spine should be touching the floor. You can lean up against the wall if you need to, or have something supporting your back, but try to keep your spine as straight as possible. If it is safe to do so, gently close your eyes and focus on the breath.

Inhale through the nose; exhale through the mouth. Drop the shoulders and unclench the jaw.

Allow a feeling of lightness to come over your body. As you focus on the feeling of lightness, send the breath all the way down to the base of the spine, into the root ball. Inhaling deeply, oxygenate the energy center at the base of your spine. Do your best to keep the breath rhythmic: inhale, oxygenate, exhale. Keep pushing that breath into the root ball until you feel calm and connected to the present moment.

Imagine a red light turns on in the root ball. Let this red light grow with each inhale as you oxygenate that energy center. The red light gets bigger and brighter. Keep this up until the red light has expanded so much that you are sitting inside it. You are fully immersed in the energy and glow of your root chakra.

Relax. Keep the breath focused. As you settle into this lovely, calm space, ask for your old programming—the programming that feels limited and restricted, the programming that makes you feel like you have to ask others for permission to live the life that you wish to live—to float up before you like a holograph. This holographic image that represents your old programming could present itself as numbers, light, a photograph, a fragment of time, or a memory. Swipe it away with your right hand. Just push it out of the bubble as it pops up. Keep swiping all of your old programming away. Push it out of that red light. Let it go.

When nothing else pops up, or when you feel you have removed all the energy that you are willing to remove in this particular setting, take another deep breath through the nose and push it out through the mouth.

Staying in that red light, turn to the left. On the left side of that red light, there is a new set of codes, images, ideas, and visions for your future. Pull them in with your left hand. These new light codes, this new software, is for the version of you that is dedicated and committed to thriving and growing and embodying the energy of the sprite.

Allow the water deities to bring fluidity and flexibility into your center of connectedness so that you were no longer rigid, stuck, or immovable. Breathe in and out as you continue to oxygenate the root. Keep pulling in with the left hand, bringing in all these new light codes. Allow the new software upgrades to happen as new patterns of energy begin resetting the frequency and vibration of your root chakra.

When you feel your upgrade is complete and no more codes appear, drop your hands and place them on your legs. Take a deep breath in through the nose and hold it for the count of five. One, two, three, four, five. Exhale.

Take another deep breath in through the nose and hold it for the count of five. One, two, three, four, five. Exhale.

One last time. Take a deep breath in through the nose, holding it for a count of five. One, two, three, four, five. Exhale. As you exhale, see that red light getting smaller and smaller. With each exhale now, the red light slowly diminishes until it blinks out. Once the root chakra's red light turns off completely, you know that your upgrade is complete.

When you are ready, wiggle your toes, roll your shoulders, and open your eyes. Rest easily knowing that you have just put in brand new codes and software, along with new memories. These are future memories—visions of what is to come. You have now finished upgrading your root chakra.

Place of Power: Ice

There are secrets hidden in the ice of the earth, secrets of our past and possible clues to our future. There is ice in Antarctica that is suspected to be millions of years old. There is ice in Alaska that is over thirty thousand years old.[4] We are surrounded by history frozen in time, hidden in the planet's ice. The stories ice has inside of it are trapped. But there is old ice, ancient ice, that is slowly melting, revealing its past, whispering down the side of mountains and along the babbling creeks.

Ice is our connection to our roots. It tells the story of where we came from and where we are going. The origins of humanity are crystallized deep inside it. We are one with the ice, even if we are unaware of it. It is interesting to think of ice as our base, a foundation we have built our history on. Many species live, love, play, build social structures, and thrive on floating slabs of ice. There is life above, below, and within the ice, much like the earth itself.

Ice has a way of bringing us back to basics, to the essential things we need. Like not freezing to death. In many ways, ice activates our survival instincts, which tend to be very creative. For the most part, modern humans haven't really had to worry much about basic survival, at least not in Western and developed countries. What we think of as survival is seriously not what our root chakra was designed to cope with, and the ice reminds us of that. It connects us to the past to show us how well-off we truly are, showing our progress through the melting permafrost. This

---

4. "How Old Is Glacier Ice?" United States Geological Survey, accessed March 24, 2022, https://www.usgs.gov/faqs/how-old-glacier-ice.

reminder allows the sprite to show us what comes next: the leap from surviving to thriving.

This is where the creative parts of your survival instincts get to kick in. You see, surviving naturally transmutes to thriving through the act of activation. This activation is a creative act. The sprite is your guide to harness this power of creativity and level up your experience. And it all starts here, in the ice. From the past to the present to the future, the ice offers it all and serves it up in one place.

The closest most of us will get to ice is snow or frost. I remember having my very first experience with snow on a freezing cold mountain in New Zealand. Honestly, I didn't like it much. It wasn't until twenty years later, when I found myself in Buffalo, New York, during a February blizzard, that I truly saw the beauty of snow and, with it, gained an appreciation for ice. It was quiet, peaceful, and calming. Well, from inside a nice warm house it was. To this day, it amazes me that tiny flakes of ice can fall from the sky and totally change the landscape without any noise at all.

In the desert, snow is magical. In Las Vegas, we are surrounded by mountains. In winter, most of them are covered by snow, which means the entire valley looks magical. To have snow on the valley floor, now that is miraculous! It does happen, it's just very unusual and we get very, very excited about it. I have been to Zion National Park during winter and seen frozen water suspended in animation on the side of mountains. I have driven on ice—not well, but safely. Ice heightens something inside of us. It triggers different responses in our mind, body, and soul. It elevates our skills and forces us to focus. And then, when we least expect it, it throws a snowball right at our faces. Creative, playful, transformative—that is the power of ice.

Spellwork

There are times in our lives when we need a break from other people's nagging and interfering energy. This could be anything from a nagging colleague or parent to an ex who just won't keep their nose out of your business. This energy usually makes us feel unsafe and a little unstable, and it can affect our self-confidence. Sometimes you just need to ice people.

Now, I should point out that this is not something harmful. In no way does this spell have karmic repercussions for you; the sprites would never allow that. It is merely a way of protecting your energy from the onslaught of others. In many ways, this spell creates a wall of ice around you so that others' energy just can't reach you—instead, it will hit the wall of ice and slip away. I have used this spell myself many times, and I have walked clients through it as well. It never ceases to amaze me just how powerful this simple spell is. But then again, the sprites have very potent magic indeed.

MAGICAL ITEMS

Paper: This could be a sheet of paper, or you could use sticky notes

A Pen: To write with

An Ice Tray: Small enough to fit in your freezer

Water: To make ice

On a piece of paper, write the names of those people whose energy you need a break from. Look at your ice tray and see how many cubes it will hold; don't write down more than one name per ice cube. If there is only one person you need to set in the deep freeze for a while, just write their name multiple times.

Next, tear the paper up so that each name is on its own slip of paper. Place one slip of paper per ice cube compartment. Then cover with water. As you pour the water over the name(s), repeat the following spell:

Sprites and ice, I call to thee, with your power assist me
Put a freeze on this energy and let this person leave me be
When the time is right and all is done
I will place them back out in the sun
Until then, they will remain behind the ice and safely away
As it is said, now it is done

Go ahead and stick the ice tray in your freezer. You might want to write a date on your calendar of when you will be ready to take the tray out. The time frame is entirely up to you.

Remember, this spell causes no harm. It is merely a form of protection for you and your energy. It allows you to feel more safe, stable, and sure about your life, your feelings, and your direction.

Mermaid Connection Exercise: Journaling with the Sprite

Over the course of this chapter, you have learned a few new tricks for how to keep things simple. You've harnessed the power of ice to make you feel a little more safe and secure and found new ways to connect with your root chakra. This chapter, like its corresponding moon phase, has an ending. You are wrapping your time with the mermaids up by bringing all you have learned back down to earth (though the mermaids and I hope you have found more flow in your root). This feels like a good time to crack open your journal and reflect on what you have learned about yourself while working with the sprite.

- Which section did you enjoy most in this chapter? Why?
- What lesson did you learn from the sprite?
- What area of your life do you need to feel more safe in?
- Where can you simplify your daily routine?
- What was your biggest "aha moment" while working through this chapter? Why is it important to where you are in your life right now?
- How will you bring the energies of play and fun into your life on a more regular basis?

Think of these prompts as ways to start the reflecting process. Do not feel limited by these questions; allow your answers to open up more discussion. Let your thoughts flow freely. There is magic in letting the words spill onto the page. Once you feel complete, move on to the cartomancy work.

Cartomancy: Page of Pentacles

Page of Pentacles

The energy of the sprite is deeply connected to the Page of Pentacles card in a tarot deck. This card is a playful card, yet it shows us how we first learn to navigate the material world. This is a childlike card with a serious edge. We know the lessons we learn here will set us up for lessons later in life, especially lessons regarding feeling safe, secure, and stable in our bodies and in the material world of things. If you are not a tarot person, you can use an oracle deck that aligns to this energy for your spread.

This is a simple spread to use when you want to receive guidance from the sprite. Place the Page of Pentacles card or an aligned oracle card faceup in front of you. This is your anchor card, also known as your significator; it grounds the energy of your inquiry and focuses it squarely on the Page of Pentacles. Pick up the rest of your deck and shuffle. While you shuffle, think of a question and bring it into your mind's eye. Some sample questions are:

- What is the best action for me to take today?
- What material things should I avoid attaching to today?
- Where can I have more fun today?
- How can I simplify my day?

You can either pull a card for each of these questions, or you can just pull one card to answer a specific question. You can also write your own questions for the sprite if you feel inclined to do so.

~

This wraps up your time with the sprite. You have done a lot of work, even if it doesn't feel like it, so be kind and gentle to yourself. When you are ready, the mermaids and I shall see you on the next page, where we have a surprise for you!

conclusion

All Good Tails Must Come to an End

If you have made it this far, you deserve a prize. Which is why I waited until the very end to tell you how to find your mermaid self. Throughout this book, I dropped hints as to which mermaid I was and which chapter was my personal chapter. Now, it is your turn. When you find out what sort of mermaid you are, your corresponding chapter will take on a deeper meaning.

So, how exactly do you find your mermaid self? It's actually pretty easy. All you need to do is find out what lunar phase you were born under. The easiest way to do that is to open up Google (or whatever search engine) you use and type in your date of birth and the words *moon phase*. Or you can search "What was the moon phase on [your date of birth]?" Either will give you the result you need.

I was born under a waxing crescent moon; so was my wife. The waxing crescent moon was discussed in chapter 2, "The Ocean

Priestess," which means that is my mermaid self. Once you've found out what moon phase you were born under, find the corresponding chapter in this book to determine your mermaid self.

I have worked with people born under many different moon phases, and I have seen firsthand how we each bring a very different approach and perspective to the people around us. In business this can be an incredible asset. It really is quite amazing that the moon phases we were born under have that much influence over the work we do. For example, I am the ocean priestess and I have partnered with people who have the water sprite archetype. Together we brought a very special energy to our projects and clients. I am older and more devotional; my collaborator was younger and more fun and energized. Somehow our mermaid selves balanced the fast/slow energy of the project we were working on and delivered mind-blowing results. The deeper you dig into your mermaid self, the more surprised you may be as you learn just how much this archetype has influenced what you do and how you show up in the world.

Each of your mermaid selves also has a corresponding time of day that will determine either when you are most creative or most productive. We have tested these times in our business with ourselves and our clients, and we are always amazed by how accurate they are. Now, of course, there will always be outliers, so do not panic if your mermaid hours do not seem to correspond to your peak flow times. Everything about this exercise is just a fun guide. Do not get too hooked on it.

Your Lunar Power Hours

New Moon: 11:00 p.m. – 4:00 a.m.

Waxing Crescent: 4:00 a.m. – 11:00 a.m.

First Quarter: 11:00 a.m. – 2:00 p.m.

Waxing Gibbous: 12:00 p.m. – 3:00 p.m.

Full Moon: 1:00 p.m. – 4:00 p.m.

Waning Gibbous: 3:00 p.m. – 6:00 p.m.

Third Quarter: 5:00 p.m. – 8:00 p.m.

Waning Crescent: 7:00 p.m. – 11:00 p.m.

I hope that nice little prize was worth making it all the way to the end of this book. Know that your personal adventure with the mermaids has only just begun. What you learned inside the pages of this book is merely an introduction to the knowledge and wisdom the mermaids have to share with you. That said, there is still so much to learn in this book. Don't just do the exercises once. Don't drop your connection to the mermaids listed in these pages just because you made it to the end. You can go deeper. Revisit the content again and again. The mermaids and I promise that each time you do, you will find something new. This book may just be an introduction, but it is far from the end of your journey. Now that you know the members of the Mermaid Pantheon, you can ask more questions, connect further, and open yourself up to explore their teachings in more profound ways.

It doesn't matter how many times I come to the mermaids, they always have something different, new, and insightful to share with me. No two experiences are ever the same. When you reread this books, perhaps you expand on the spells, create your own rituals, or even find a new and exciting way to do the healings.

Or perhaps you begin to incorporate the lunar work in this book with your other moon phases studies. How magical would it be to combine the astrology of the moon phases with your mermaid energy? I feel we have only just scratched the surface of what is possible by calling the mermaids into our lives through a daily and intentional process. I know I will be using the contents of this book in my priestess work.

Parting is always bittersweet, but for now our time together has come to an end. We wish you well on your journey.

—Leeza and the Mermaids xxxooo

P. S. I would love to see how you are using this book and how it is inspiring your own spiritual work. Don't forget to follow and tag me on Instagram so I can see how the mermaids are infusing themselves into our daily life. You can find me at @theleezarob ertson.

Recommended Reading

Astrology for Real Life: A Workbook for Beginners by Theresa Reed

Awaken Your Inner Goddess: Practical Tools for Self-Care, Emotional Healing, and Self-Realization by Dara Goldberg

The Body of the Goddess: Sacred Wisdom in Myth, Landscape, and Culture by Rachel Pollack

Deeply into the Bone: Re-Inventing Rites of Passage by Ronald L. Grimes

If Women Rose Rooted: A Life-Changing Journey to Authenticity and Belonging by Sharon Blackie

Jailbreaking the Goddess: A Radical Revisioning of Feminist Spirituality by Lasara Firefox Allen

Lunar Abundance: Cultivating Joy, Peace, and Purpose Using the Phases of the Moon by Ezzie Spencer

Mermaid Tarot by Leeza Robertson

Mysteries of the Dark Moon: The Healing Power of the Dark Goddess by Demetra George

The Mythic Moons of Avalon: Lunar & Herbal Wisdom from the Isle of Healing by Jhenah Telyndru

Priestess: Ancient Spiritual Wisdom for Modern Sacred Women by Julie Parker

Rise Sister Rise: A Guide to Unleashing the Wise, Wild Woman Within by Rebecca Campbell

Waking the Witch: Reflections on Women, Magic, and Power by Pam Grossman

Wicca Moon Magic: A Wiccan's Guide and Grimoire for Working Magic with Lunar Energies by Lisa Chamberlain

You Are A Goddess: Working with the Sacred Feminine to Awaken, Heal, and Transform by Sophie Bashford